GW00859410

Way Stations on the Path to Awakening
Deep Love, Hope and Faith

Isaura Barrera

BALBOA.
PRESS
A DIVISION OF HAY HOUSE

Balboa Press books may be ordered through booksellers or by contacting:

Balboa Press
A Division of Hay House
1663 Liberty Drive
Bloomington, IN 47403
www.balboapress.com
1 (877) 407-4847

About the Cover Image

The depiction of a gift represents the gift of friendship that initiated and shaped my journey. The ring design is chosen because it captures the essence of that journey. It depicts the heart and hands claddagh ring design with a circle of shining stones threaded through it. The claddagh represents the deep friendship that inspired my journey and inspires me still. The circle of shining stones depicts the Spirit that threaded through it while my friend was physically present and continues to thread through it now (Ring and image by My Irish Jeweler; www.myirishjeweler.com).

Print information available on the last page.

ISBN: 978-1-9822-2446-2 (sc)
ISBN: 978-1-9822-2447-9 (hc)
ISBN: 978-1-9822-2448-6 (e)

Library of Congress Control Number: 2019903482

Balboa Press rev. date: 04/09/2019

DEDICATION

For you, my beloved friend
amor de mi alma, anam cara,
Distillations from our loving
-- God's gift of Infinite Light and Love sent to me through you --
GRACIAS!

And to all others who have in ways small and large brought sustenance and substance to my journey. Some I've met face to face, others I know only through their written work. Thank you.

Contents

About this Book

A few words about two aspects of this book are perhaps necessary. First, it is distinct from my earlier book, *Beloved's Gift: Following Soul's Song into Love, Hope and Joy* in two ways. *Beloved's Gift* was primarily published for a single reader, my beloved friend who inspired it. It was also, in a sense, published prematurely. Though I had no clear idea why, I felt an underlying sense of urgency as I wrote it and, consequently, rushed my writing. As it turned out, it published only a few months before my beloved friend passed away. In that sense it was not premature at all. In another sense though it remained less than what it would have been had I taken more time to develop its themes and format.

There is less urgency in my writing now and I no longer write for just one person. My words are offered with the wider hope that they may offer inspiration and some clues to others seeking a palpable presence of love, faith and hope, both as mystery that embraces and frees at the heart of earth's darkness and as light that clarifies and sustains.

Additionally, I have added new material as my journey continued to an intuited yet unanticipated fruition: the gift initially received from a human beloved now fully unwrapped as gift from Divine Beloved.

Second, in contrast to more typical memoirs, "it does not pretend to record experiences but [rather] to describe places to which the reader is invited."[1] I do not, as one editor insisted I should, recount anecdotes of where I was or what I was doing to anchor my reflections. Unfortunately, or perhaps fortunately, that is in keeping with neither my intent nor my skill set. Though inspired by the development of a deep friendship with a human beloved, the thoughts I share do not focus specifically on that friendship. Rather, they focus on the insights that marked the inner spiritual landscapes I traversed as I unwrapped its gift. Parker Palmer describes this type of writing as an "unfolding of what's going on inside me."[2]

I have come to see my writing as a type of *Lectio Divina*, a traditional Christian practice in which the words of scripture are seen "as God's living words spoken to our hearts in this moment."[3] My words are rooted in seeing my experiences as Infinite Light and Love spoken in and to my heart.[4] They are offered as a type of meditative map to invite readers to do the same.

Several factors influenced this choice of an inner focus over a focus on the external landscape of the human friendship that inspired and accompanied me. First, by nature and disposition I have always found the deepest meaning and significance in interior rather than exterior reality. Though the two can never be totally separated, the happenings in my inner world almost always trump those in my exterior world, influencing how I interpret and respond to that world. I can recall almost exactly how I felt or what I was thinking at particular times. I find it much more difficult to recall where I was physically or what I was doing.

Another reason for my choice of an inner focus came from the friend who inspired my journey. He was in many ways an extremely private individual, seldom willing to talk about our friendship in particular or spirituality in general. With gentle respect, which I did not always understand, he allowed me to explore the inner landscapes opened by our friendship on my own.

Look to God, not me" was a common refrain from my friend. For a long time I believed it was meant to turn me away from the "us" I so deeply desired. It took a while to recognize that this response was about much more than humility or, worse, about his rejection of what I experienced. Only as I traversed the inner landscapes traced in this book did I begin to realize his intent was actually the opposite. It was to turn me toward the deeper reality within which our friendship rested and from which it drew its shape and its strength.

Through his silence, my friend prompted me to become aware of aspects of myself that, though somehow triggered by him or at times mirrored in him, did not come from him. These were not disconnected from the external reality of our relationship, of course, but neither were they dependent on it. As Byron Katie has said: "The truth is that your partner is your mirror. You are always what you judge him to be in the moment."[5] This was not an easy truth for me to learn. I so wanted the truth to be that if only my friend would do or say something different all would be OK with us, and more importantly perhaps, within me.

Over time, I became aware that it was not what my friend did or said that determined my experience. He had, in fact, done and said many of the same things when we'd first met many years before. Like the princess in the Princess Bride movie, however, I'd not really heard the truth behind them. John O'Donohue echoes this point in this marvelous book *Anam Cara*: "You can search long years in lonely places, far outside yourself. Yet, the whole time, this love is but a few inches away from you. It is at the edge of your soul, but you have been blind to its presence."[6]

Only after I reconnected with my friend did I finally recognize that what makes all the difference is *how* we hear and perceive not *what* we hear and perceive. I know now that my journey was and continues to be defined not by the particularities of a single friendship but by the process of opening to and reclaiming my soul's song of love, hope and faith to which that friendship reawakened me.

Prologue:

SOUL'S SONG REAWAKENED

"...*one day, unexpected and unhoped for, the world we had thought irretrievably lost may be returned to us. In a moment of insight—a sudden opening of the heart—we may glimpse again the mysterious reality we took for granted as children"—and hear our soul sing once again*
(I. Zaleski)

The idea that each of us carry deep within our souls a particular song sung just for us has always resonated for me. It is an idea that I first found when I read about communities that believe that every baby comes into this earth with their own unique song, a song that gives voice to and sustains undying love, hope and faith.[7] It is said that female elders in these communities gather around an expectant mother prior to a birth to listen for the baby's song that they might sing it to welcome the child into the world at birth.

I like to think of this song as the voice of Infinite Light and Love echoing through human heart and mind.[8] It is a soul song I believe we hear clearly though perhaps not explicitly in childhood. Unfortunately, it is also a song we all too often relegate to fairytales or forget entirely as we start to grow up and external reality mutes it through betrayal or abuse. At least it was so for me.

Song First Sung

I remember hearing my own soul's song as a child. I did not think of it as such at the time, of course, but I felt its joy and heard its melody in words said to me, in loving gazes, and in the acceptance of others as I offered my love to them.[9] It sounded all around me, weaving the melodies of love, hope and faith into every aspect of the creation I experienced. I remember the wild and joyful believing that stirred in me as I heard them. Much later I found such believing strikingly and whimsically described: "…to believe in God is to know purple jelly beans could hatch into ostriches and tulip bulbs break into blooms as big as rooms or even rabbits could produce humans out of hats…."[10]

Song Lost

I remember too when other sounds, dissonant and off-key, started to dim the sounds of my soul's song. Gradually, in the face of others' definitions of reality and my own limited understandings, I relegated my soul's song—and much of the love, hope and faith it affirmed—to the realm of make-believe and childhood dreams. I began measuring reality based on external judgments valued by others. The realm of Infinite Light and Love, in which were rooted the love, hope and faith my soul sang, became a reality imagined more than experienced.

In ways small and large I started to perceive that realm as separate and contrary to my lived reality. I placed the two apart, calling one heaven and the other, earth. I would not have described it in that way then. I, and others around me, would have said I was merely growing up. Yet, looking back now, I realize that what I had actually done was to disconnect soul from self, perhaps not consciously yet systematically all the same. I came to see Infinite Light and Love as childish, wildly trustful believing that could not be in the real world. I put it to one side (in heaven) and put finite light and love—adult rational believing—to the other (on earth).

Finally, there came a time when I could no longer reconcile my lived reality on earth with the love, hope and faith my soul sang. "It's too good to be true. Perhaps after we die but certainly not here and not now. Look around you. Don't be foolish. Realism is necessary for survival. Life isn't a fairytale...." The words went on and on, once heard from others then firmly entrenched in my own mind. The voices of Infinite Light and Love—"God is good. You are deeply loved. Every hair on your head is counted. Ask and you will receive...."—faded into almost soundless whispers articulated only in the depths of my soul.

My doubting grew and flowered. The world of my five senses, which I'd found so filled with wonder, became opaque, seeming to confirm the unreality of my original intuitions and beliefs.

I started to "grow up," and stopped hearing my soul's song. Its melody continued to echo, but only in the fairytales I loved, and, sometimes, in deeply longed for but all too infrequent moments of joy and acceptance. Every now and then I'd experience something or connect deeply with someone and it would all seem to come back, only to disappear again. My believing fell increasingly into a box labeled "make-believe," something that could never really happen, not here on earth.

In a desperate attempt to come to terms with reality as others told me it must be, I fashioned a homemade self (i.e., ego) that was more socially acceptable (i.e., grown up) and a heaven that held the Light and Love I'd known but was somewhere other than where I was. Later, as an adult with no memory of my original pain or of my confusion about how Infinite Light and Love could be actually present amid and through what happened and what others said, I turned around and castigated myself for my alienation from my soul.

As time continued, I struggled to hold on to my believing, building a wall to protect Infinite Light and Love and the deep love, trusting hope and unimaginable KNOWING it brought me from the assaults of an everyday reality that was now too small to contain either. Almost imperceptibly, that wall thickened. Infinite Light and Love (heaven) and earth, once a single reality, split into two ever more irreconcilable realities. When I heard whispers of my soul's song with its message of never-ending love, hope and faith I reminded myself that I was no longer a child. (Interestingly, the homemade self[11] I constructed literally could not sing on key.) In the resulting emptiness, I was left feeling abandoned, separate, and alone.

Song Re-awakened

It took a long time and the unexpected reconnection with a dear friend for me to realize that this separation of "heaven" and "earth" was not, as some say, about a pretentious and selfish ego striking out on its own out of a need to seek power and self-gratification. It was in reality about a wounded heart unable to sustain its perception of the presence of Infinite Light and Love on this earth in the face of experiences that assaulted it and an immature ego doing its best to keep me alive.

Though soul songs can reawaken in many ways, for me it happened when one day I opened a book whose words about friendship quite literally struck a chord. Suddenly I could hear my soul's song of love, hope and faith once again in all its clarity. I reached out to reconnect with that song. As I did, I stepped through a doorway that led to the journey I share in this book.

Such doorways are, I believe, quite literally openings into the innermost ground of our being where we meet and are met by Infinite Light and Love[12] and, where we literally find heaven on earth (i.e., unending love, hope and faith). Perhaps these doorways are all around us, awaiting only our recognition. That is what some cultures and traditions believe when they affirm that there are sacred times and places where the veil between the physical world and the spiritual nonmaterial world thins to allow us to experience both as one.

Sometimes, I think, these doorways come in quite ordinary ways. At other times they may come in the form of an unexpected event or experience. At still other times a doorway may appear, as it did for me, in the form of a faithful friend returned. In whatever form they come, all doorways have one thing in common: they provide us with an opening into the space where we can once again resonate to the melody of our soul's song. The doorway that opened for me was a totally unexpected one. I read a book about friendship and remembered a friend—two ordinary experiences—and found myself standing at an opening through which the Infinite Light and Love I'd once known in my soul's song beckoned me once again—an extraordinary experience.

Looking back, I can discern the signs pointing me toward that door. For as long as I can remember, stories of deep friendship have intrigued me. I've always been drawn to such stories, whether make-believe fairytales, fictional romances, or real-life stories. I have always been especially drawn to the stories of Christian mystics like Heloise and Abelard and Clare and Francis, whose human love affirmed the presence of Infinite Light and Love on earth.

Only recently, however, have I recognized the common theme that threads across these stories. Whether fictional or real, the characters in those stories, like Jesus' disciples in Christian scripture, possessed what I vaguely recalled from early childhood and desperately longed to regain: a sense of gifted love so strong and so deep it quite literally brings heaven to earth, making sacredness and miracles as palpable as trees and cats. Just imagination? That's what I'd been told and what I'd come to believe. What I discovered as I stepped through the doorway my renewed friendship opened for me was that it is only such love that is truly real.

From the start, my reawakened soul's song challenged my adopted make-believe belief that Infinite Light and Love here and now was only a child's dream. As the unexpected return of an old friend brought back memories of the innocence and joy both mirrored and celebrated when we'd first met, visceral memories of Infinite Light and Love also awoke. It was not, however, as simple as just returning to where I'd been. I'd learned what the intervening years had taught me all too well. There were times when I wondered if it wasn't all just one more illusion, too good to be true.

It was then that I started to reflect intentionally on the path that unfolded before me. As I did, a series of significant stopping points or way stations evolved organically as I was brought up short, sometimes by more joy than I imagined could be and other times by unexpected challenges that confused and frustrated me. While on the exterior my renewed friendship was extremely ordinary (e.g., my friend and I talked every few days and met only occasionally), beneath that ordinary exterior was an extraordinary spiritual landscape that restored my soul's song and led me into the undying love, hope and faith it affirmed. It is that spiritual landscape that I share through my reflections on the way stations of my journey.

Introduction:

ANATOMY OF AN INNER JOURNEY

Love opened the door; hope kept it open;
faith gives me the courage to walk through

VISUAL MAP

LOVE ⟶ ***HOPE*** ⟶ ***FAITH***

COMMITTING TO LOVE: JOURNEY'S BEGINNING

Choosing Connection	***Choosing Light***	***Choosing Miracles***

HARVESTING THE WONDERS: FAIRYTALE COME TRUE

Finding Priceless Treasures	***Incredible Truths***	***Transformation***

UNMAPPED BELIEVING: JOB'S DILEMMA

Halfway to the Miracle	***Crying out day and night***	***With Trembling Heart***

THREE STEPS FORWARD, TWO STEPS BACK: MOVING TO THE MUSIC

Contradictions transcended	***Metanoia***	***Dancing***

SONG UNENDING: AFTER HAPPILY EVER AFTER

Returning To Galilee	***Seeing Rightly***	***Co-creating Song***

This book has a double purpose: to describe an inner journey inspired by deep friendship and to offer that description as a meditative map for others as they travel their own journeys. The various stopping places or way stations on which I reflect trace the path carved out by the song of love, hope and faith sung by my soul and evoked by my renewed friendship.

It all began with reading John O'Donohue's *Anam Cara*. The words I read reminded me that I'd once known an *anam cara*—a beloved friend—such as he described. That remembrance inspired me to call that friend, with whom I'd not been in touch for many years. The joy of my reconnection with my friend—recognized now through the lens of *anam cara*—reawakened a love, hope and faith long dormant within me. It opened a door for me through which I glimpsed Infinite Light and Love as both concretely and spiritually real.

It did not take long to realize that my journey followed a spiral path, from love to hope to faith and back again. When love's direction became uncertain and its reality doubtful, hope emerged, keeping love's door open and sustaining me through the doubts and fear that blurred love's colors and muted its music. Some times, though, the voices of accumulated pain threatened to silence both love and hope: "Run; protect yourself" "Remember past hurts." "Are you nuts?" "All things may be possible for God, but do you see God now?" "Maybe in heaven, but not here or now." Faith came then, something solid, beyond mental convictions and rote beliefs used to control or hold at bay all that would disturb, opening my heart once again to the reality before me even when it didn't look or feel as I wanted.

These spiral dynamics of love, hope, and faith marked the twist and turns of my journey, sometimes conforming to and confirming my hopes and dreams and exceeding all I dared to hope and dream at times, and sometimes unexpectedly challenging those very hopes and dreams. Gradually I was led into a journey far longer and much deeper than I'd ever imagined or expected.

Along the way, there were pause points or way stations shaped by the joys I celebrated as well as the challenges with which I struggled. Each way station evolved organically as I sought the meaning of where I was and what was happening. Each was both preparation for and foretaste of the next.

The first two way stations—Committing to Love: Journey's Beginning and Harvesting the Wonders: Fairytale Come True—came in the early days of my renewed friendship with my beloved friend. They were occasioned by the deep joy I felt as our friendship reawakened me to my soul's song of love, hope and faith.

In contrast, the next two—Unmapped Believing: Job's Dilemma and Three Steps Forward and Two Back: Moving to the Music—were grounded in my efforts to come to terms with the confusion and frustration I experienced when my recovered friendship did not proceed as I expected or wanted. These continued as my friend and I faced the challenges of sustaining our friendship even when it did not conform to our expectations. The last way station—Song Unending: After Happily Ever After—began as I faced the challenge of continuing my journey without my friend's physical presence. It is one that remains in progress

At each way station, I reflected on my experience and sought resonance between it and the greatest story of love and friendship I know: the story of Jesus and his disciples, both male and female. After all, if that story was all it claimed to be, I should be able to find the resonance between it and my own experiences of love and friendship. And that resonance could both support and inspire me along the way.

Though admittedly unique to me in many ways, I've nevertheless chosen to share my journey in the belief that the value of others' experience "is to give us hope, not to tell us how or whether to proceed."[13] It is my hope that any who have found or are finding themselves facing similar way stations, be they triggered by friendship or other circumstances, may find in my words an invitation to reaffirm, or perhaps affirm for the first time, their soul's song of love, hope and faith and unwrap the gift it bears for them.

Committing To Love:

JOURNEY'S BEGINNING

"..it is like being awakened to a dimension of yourself that has been there all this time, flowing like an underground river, although until now it has gone undetected."
(D. Michie)

While joyous in many ways, the first months of reconnection with my friend were also times when inner reflection often seemed the only option. We lived in different states, saw each other only once or twice a year and talked with varying frequency on the phone, sometimes not for several weeks at a time. Nevertheless, the energy that had drawn us together so long ago kept us together now, inviting a commitment to the connection, light and miracles that emerged from our growing love.

Choosing Connection

"We all need such friends who image God's love and acceptance to us. They give us the courage to risk loving a God we cannot see."
(T. Green)

Central to my choosing connection was the recognition and reawakening of what O'Donohue calls an "ancient belonging," a sense of relationship that seems to be beyond time and space.[14] For me, this recognition was marked first by a sense of being recalled by love's gaze and leaping out into its embrace. The challenge of running into unanticipated storms followed soon after, however, shaking that recognition and challenging my initial joy. It was as I negotiated that challenge I think that I first recognized this initial way station.

Recalled by Love's Gaze

I still remember the visceral sensation of a space opening up in my chest when I first opened myself to my friend's loving gaze. It happened at one of our first meetings as we embraced in greeting. Though it only lasted a few minutes, I still remember the shift I felt in my heart as I let myself fall back past closed doors and into all the dreams that lay dormant within me. My first response was pure joy. I felt I'd found a long lost beloved home, a reality I had come to believe couldn't really exist. I felt myself drift into the stars like an astronaut outside a space ship hearing the SNAP! of the line that connects him to his ship. Awe-filled, I let myself float on the wonder of it all.

Soon after, on the heels of that joy, came a second response. Deep fear stirred within me as my mind questioned my heart: "What if you're wrong?" "What if it's all in your head?" "It's too good to be true." I could not silence those questions even as I yearned to do so. Fears and memories I'd thought banished reappeared. Even so, I could not set aside the fact that, when I let myself, I felt a joy that I knew without a doubt echoed God's voice. A door long shut had opened. I knew I never wanted to close it again. I needed to commit to the connection I felt. I'd lived long enough without this soul-deep joy to know that life without it wasn't really life at all.

Nevertheless, a silent grief and almost-terror gnawed at the edges of my joy. I was not unaware of innocence lost, of joy turning to confusion, of trust betrayed into shame. I wondered: if I let go and fell back into joy in total trust and abandon, would it hold this time? Or would it vanish, as it had done so many times before, throwing me back into "reality?" Could I be safe this time?

Nevertheless, an assurance of love and safety unlike any I'd ever known threaded itself through the questions as my commitment to connection strengthened. My newly reawakened soul's song brought continued assurance of what I'd stopped believing could be truly real. All my wanderings away from God's delight and wonder came into plain sight, contrasting sharply with my sense of gift. Perhaps that is one of the key aspects of right loving—its ability to gently yet undeniably show us the truth of our being.

In my newly rediscovered friendship, love's gaze—the gaze of Infinite Light and Love—found me, like scripture's woman at the well, in the heat of day and in the midst of my deepest thirst, trying to draw inanimate water from wells of my own construction. Like Jesus in that story, Infinite Light and Love called me to re-connect with the reality for which I actually thirsted. I reread the familiar story and imagined it as my own story.

Scripture Meditation: The Woman at the Well (*John 4: 7-15)*

> *Parched with thirst, I had gone to the well to draw water to sustain me for one more day. It had become a familiar pattern. I was so tired. I wished sometimes that it could be easier, that I didn't have to go so far during the hottest part of the day. I longed to go with someone but I walked alone, without any real belief that things would change. Then, one day, there was a man at the well. When I got closer I lowered my eyes, never expecting what happened next. He looked straight at me without shame, as no one (not even myself) had in a very long time. I still remember the sudden visceral sensation of a space opening in my chest and literally feeling myself fall past the closed doors behind which I'd shut my true self so long ago.*
>
> *His gaze stirred memories I'd forgotten were even there, re-membering the parts of myself that for so long had been judged shameful and unacceptable. I felt innocence and trust. These remained whole, buried in my heart's core, sheltered zealously behind the only barriers it knew how to erect: doubt and fear.*
>
> *In that moment, I raised my eyes to meet his, and remembered a time when I had not thirsted as I did now. Like the sight of something or someone once fiercely loved and then lost, I felt both joy and pain in the seeing. Intimations of grief intermingled with a joy deeper than any I'd known for a very long time. I was so far from who I had once been, from who I authentically was. My heart's home seemed so far away and yet so close. I couldn't help wondering the*

impossible: could I become whole once more? Could I believe once again what I'd given up believing was ever really true? Could heaven be right here and right now, within my reach? I knew I had to find out.

Leaping Out of Homemade Boats

Even though nothing much changed externally, as my connection deepened I began to believe the fullness of love's promise. Led by a vision stronger than logic and deeper than reason, more powerful than old habits and beliefs, I felt that anything—even walking on water—was possible. All doubts and fears seemed to vanish, leaving only joy in their wake. I felt sure love could surmount any challenge that might appear.

I remembered Peter's story of leaping out of his boat to meet his friend across the water during a storm. I'd always wondered how Peter had really felt when he saw his beloved friend across the water. Without knowing why or how, he'd leapt out of the boat in answer to his own urgent desire to be with—and in—Love Incarnate. I imagined he'd done so not out of impulse or even faith, but out of love so sheer and trust so deep that there was no room for any other response. His wild and trusting leap out of the boat to meet Jesus in the dark and on the water captured the sense of my own response to the reawakening of my soul's song. It was not hard to imagine myself doing the same.

<u>Scripture Meditation: Peter, Jumping Out of the Boat</u> *(Matthew 14: 23-29)*

I felt such terror during the storm. Just as it seemed I'd finally found all I'd ever wanted, here I was, apart from Love Incarnate and surely about to die. The sea seemed rougher than I'd ever seen it before. It seemed

> *intent on overturning the boat, on overturning my newfound reality. Of course I knew that I should be stronger, have more faith. Of course I knew I should believe. But I'd seen storms just like this one before. I knew all too well that boats capsized despite all efforts and worse, despite all God's love.*
>
> *Then, just at the moment of my worst fear, I looked into the distance and there he was, the friend I'd come to love. He was walking calmly across the water as if nothing was wrong. I couldn't believe my eyes but my heart knew: it was him and there was nothing wrong, not anymore. I yelled out for his assurance, "Is it really you? Invite me to come to you." When he said "Come on over," I leapt up out of the boat, how could I not? There was no thinking, no self-consciousness and no doubt, only a deep KNOWING. My heart soared and my feet barely touched the water. I was, literally, in heaven on earth.*

Running Into Storms

Even as my soul's song grew stronger and my commitment to connection deepened, the tension between how I'd envisioned my rediscovered friendship and how it was actually taking form remained. I became conscious of the thickness of the walls I'd so carefully erected. Once intended to protect me, I could now see that they only separated me from the parts of reality and myself I feared discovering were not real.

I knew this place. It was a familiar one. I'd been here before: praying fervently yet continuing to sink into my fears and doubts. Its familiarity pushed old triggers and turned me back to all the homemade strategies I'd concocted to stay afloat. Like entering a place where once my soul was wounded, my body and my mind remembered old explosions. I thought I'd defused all the landmines only to discover that it was one thing to defuse them, and another thing entirely to dare to unearth the treasures and the secrets they'd guarded for so long.

I ran headfirst into shards of my splintered self. Some I'd buried because I believed they were only fairytales, "too good to be true," never to be realized on earth. These were carefully protected, like gifts one must never unwrap for fear they'll turn to dust in the sun's light. Others, also deeply buried, were shameful or imperfect, never good enough be fully shared with God (or anyone else), not to be opened for fear the sun's light would only make them more real.

Invariably, as had happened so many times before, the hand of Love reached out to me in the form of a story I came across. It was a story about a mystic and a philosopher lost in the forest during a severe storm. The philosopher stares up at each lightening strike, marveling at its power and brilliance. The mystic keeps his eye firmly on ground. The moral of the story lies in its message about each. The philosopher is blinded after each episode of lightening, losing sight of the path before him. The mystic, in contrast, sees the path more clearly in its light.

At the same time I remembered the words a Buddhist friend had once told me: "Do not treasure it. Do not reject it. Become intimate with it."[15] Slowly I learned that what was required to focus on my path was not personal ability or willpower. Rather it was alignment with the power of Infinite Light and Love, always within me to tell me what needed to be done, and always without and beyond, to provide all that I could not.[16]

I turned to the second half of Peter's story. Peter too had become frightened and had started to sink after he'd leapt out of the boat and walked toward his Beloved. I imagined his experience of losing trust and starting to sink through the lens of my own fading trust.

Scripture Meditation: Peter, Sinking *(Matthew 14:30-32)*

There I was, full of joy, walking on water toward my Beloved! Talk about God making the impossible possible. But then my gaze shifted. I took my focus off the love that drew me. Doubts and fears broke in. Could this really be? Wasn't walking on water impossible, only a fairytale? I suddenly noticed how strong the wind was and how powerless I was. Who was I to think that I could walk on water? Hadn't I learned better than to defy the voices that told me to think before I leapt?

I felt myself starting to sink. Logic's voice shouted at me about the laws of gravity and the properties of water. I scrambled to maintain my equilibrium but couldn't help asking, "Had innocence and trust led me astray once more as they'd seemed to in the past? Had they brought me out here only to teach me not to jump (literally) to conclusions?" With each passing moment, I felt myself sinking further.

Surely it couldn't be God's will that I be out here, walking on water, could it? If it was God's will, I wouldn't be sinking, would I? I felt more confused and scared with every passing moment. I almost forgot to look up to see Love Incarnate still gazing at me. I was almost too ashamed to see, much less grasp, the love and acceptance held out to me in that gaze. I realized then just how much I needed to choose light even when I could not see it.

Choosing Light

When every pain, every separation, is allowed to remain—that is, exist in the fullness of feeling—then the light it is made of begins to emerge. (J. Shulman)

I soon discovered that, apart from love's light, love's connection cannot *be*. Without choosing light, love's connection inevitably fades. I realized that I needed to reflect more explicitly on light. I started with reflecting on reclaiming my soul's song whose notes always brought light. These reflections in turn led to reflections on unbinding my hope and then on walking between maps.

Reclaiming Soul's Song

I had separated heaven, Infinite Light and Love, from earth a long time ago. Now, through the ebbs and flows of friendship's journey, I was learning to heal that separation and recognize that Infinite Light and Love—heaven—was never really separate from earth. Though often overshadowed by the illusions of my homemade self,[17] Infinite Light and Love nevertheless remained, standing guard to protect me from further pain and loss. I realized I needed to learn to negotiate these shadowed times. The image of wrestling with God emerged for me as I struggled to make Infinite Light and Love real—or perhaps as Infinite Light and Love struggled to make me real—in the very places where I could not sense any intimations of either.

I was first captured by the image of wrestling when I read a story in *The Last Temptation of Christ*.[18] In this story Mary and Joseph seek counsel from a renowned wise rabbi in a nearby town because Jesus has been restless and unable to sleep. The wise man asks Jesus what is troubling him. Jesus responds that he is wrestling with God. After a bit more discussion, the rabbi tells Mary and Joseph to leave Jesus with him for a while. During their time together the wise rabbi talks to Jesus about God. He tells him that God is a friend whom we can trust, and teaches him to take quiet walks with Jesus. After some time, the story says, Jesus is healed and can sleep once again. Kazantzakis ends the story by saying that after a number of weeks Jesus returns home *where he becomes the best carpenter Nazareth has ever known*. In this subtle fashion, Kazantzakis tells us that, once Jesus stopped wrestling with God, he also stopped short of his unearthing his deepest truth. He actualized one vocation, being a carpenter, at the expense of his much deeper vocation of becoming prophet and messiah.

I remembered the message of that story now. When we do not wrestle with God (if we are indeed called to do so), we fail to unveil angels that walk in the very places where Infinite Light and Love seems most absent. So, within each moment of confusion and fear, despair and hopelessness, I wrestled to unveil angels: bright and shining truths that revealed a bit more of the light that redeemed my self into full being and returned it to its rightful embodied and whole-hearted joy.

I'd never thought however that, as Infinite Light and Love flowed in, so much of what I'd come to rely on would be thrown into question. Interestingly, much later I read the following in the Gospel of Thomas: "When they find [what they seek], they will be disturbed…"[19]

A second story of wrestling came to mind as my own "wrestling" with the challenges before me started to transform me: the scripture story of Jacob wrestling with an angel. It was not hard to imagine myself in his place as he was leaving the places he'd known for a new place to live. It is said that it was then, at night when he must have felt the most alone, that he found himself wrestling with an angel, though he did not recognize it as such at first. I felt I knew what it might be like to wrestle in the dark with an angel we cannot recognize.

Scripture Meditation: Jacob Wrestling with an Angel *(Genesis 32: 24-29)*

I was never the same after that night, the night the angel came. Of course I didn't know him as an angel at first. I recognized nothing of God in him. I only knew that I wrestled with something fearsome. It came like a shadow, blotting out all light. Even the moon seemed to disappear.

They say I wrestled him. That makes it sound like I was strong and courageous. I wasn't. At least not in the way it's usually meant, acting with fearless confidence. What energy I had came from desperation and stubbornness. I'd already lost my home once. Now, so close to regaining it, I couldn't turn back. I couldn't lose my home again. So I wrestled and hung on for dear life (literally), at once refusing to let go and resisting his embrace.

In the wrestling I kept trying to feel just what or who this was I wrestled with. Then, as dawn began to break, I wondered, could this be of God? I couldn't let go until I knew. I felt my hip almost break as I stretched to stay connected and not let go. Was I being pulled down to earth, away from the heaven I'd always sought? Or up into heaven, away from all I desired here on earth?

Before I could think, this force asked to be released. I couldn't, not without knowing. So I cried out to be blessed. And it was then that I recognized it as an angel and my reality was renamed, for once we wrestle with an angel heaven and earth embrace and become one. Light broke on the horizon, flaring all around. I was never the same after that night.

Unbinding Hope

Angels unveiled more of what I barely even dared to dream. I believed I was finally home. Valleys of darkness morphed into mountaintops full of light as my certainty of Infinite Light and Love and my friend's acceptance and love strengthened. I couldn't believe there was anything more. I wanted to stay there forever.

I feared returning to the valleys, where fog crept in so unexpectedly, obscuring the light and confusing my sense of direction. It was through another's words that I first started to learn how to find light even in the valleys. In her book *Faith* Sharon Salzberg differentiates between true hope and " fixated hope." She describes the latter as "one of the most subtle ways fear can bind us, so quietly we hardly know to call it fear."[20]

As I faced the discontinuity between where I wanted to be (i.e., on the mountaintop) and where I didn't want to be (i.e., in the valley), I realized just how easily my hope became fixated. I'd start to hope I could remain on the mountaintop, then almost imperceptibly, I would become frustrated when that desired possibility did not materialize how or when I wanted. I'd start to hope even harder without realizing that, in so doing, I was fixating my hope, tying it ever more fiercely to desired forms, anticipated moments, and longed-for outcomes.

Initially open, my hope would thus become constricted, "circumscribing [my] happiness"[21] and strangling my ability to go beyond where I already was. I couldn't understand that a vast reality beyond anything I could conceive waited to unfold outside the limitations imposed by my now fear-bound hope. Through the change of circumstances and the wash of my own terror I couldn't sustain my trust that the love and light I so treasured would endure.

Only with agonizing slowness did I learn that perfect mountaintop moments were not meant to be static frozen visions, enshrined and held inviolate. They were instead meant to inspire me to step outside familiar maps into a greater and grander reality.

I realized that my reality—my self—was being transformed as I untangled my hope from the narrow thoughts and expectations that limited it.

It was not hard to find a story that connected with my experience. It was the story of Peter, John and James experiencing a bright mountaintop joy they'd never expected. I envisioned Peter's experiences of that bright joy from my own perspective.

Scripture Meditation: Transfiguration *(Luke 9: 28-33)*

> *There it was, that shining beyond-belief reality I'd experienced before, when I walked on water and then again as I was pulled to safety. I'd thought I'd never experience it again yet here it was. I wanted to enshrine it, keep it pure and untouched, with me always. I'd lost it once; I couldn't bear to lose it again.*
>
> *I wanted to stay there, just like that, wrapped within it. But it was over almost before I fully realized it was there. I didn't understand. There was so much I did not understand. Why did it all have to keep changing? When it got good—when we finally reached the mountaintop -- why couldn't we stay there? We had come so far, wasn't it precisely for this? What else could there be?*
>
> *Dared I hope deeply and freely enough to let things unfold in their own way, in their own time? Could I remember and continue to KNOW, even as I returned to valleys of unknowing once again? Could I unbind my hope and receive its full promise?*

Walking Between Maps

The core plot of the story I told myself in times of loss and disillusionment when nothing was as I wanted was one adopted and nurtured by a homemade self determined to protect me from ever again experiencing the depth of pain and shame I'd once experienced. It was a story that kept returning whenever my path deviated from familiar and predictable patterns.

At such times, I felt caught "between maps," between a new reality that promised heaven on earth (though I could not quite see how) and my old reality full of familiar stories and patterns. The former promised love, hope and faith beyond any I could imagine. The latter offered me validation if not love, security if not hope and certainty if not faith.

Full of promise and simultaneously fraught with danger, these times between maps tested my patience. Like Lazarus, I felt entombed at times, with no hope of resurrection. Promises of what might be but was not yet heightened my frustration. Echoes of long ago betrayals raged within me, telling me to close my heart's doors once again. No one came the last time, these echoes said; no one will come now either. All evidence for KNOWING the truth my soul sang seemed to vanish.

I yearned to shake loose of expectations and walk unfamiliar paths without fear. I struggled to untie fear's tethers and faith-fully open to Infinite Light and Love's presence even as I stared into valleys that seemed to have become canyons with unseen and unforeseeable bottoms. I wanted to keep choosing light. Miraculously, when I did, the KNOWING somehow remained. When I dared to remain between maps, the steadfast presence of a light and love beyond any I could imagine shone brightly once again.

I turned to a familiar scripture story: two apostles after the crucifixion on the road to Emmaus, disheartened, talking about the loss of Jesus and the dreams he'd carried for them. It was all too easy for me at this time to enter into their story of shattered dreams. I imagined myself walking beside them.

Scripture Meditation: Road to Emmaus (Part I) *(Luke 24: 13-24)*

> *So there we were, all that we had believed and sacrificed for seemingly ended. The person we had placed all our hopes on was gone. The life we'd hoped to share was now no longer possible. It seemed there was nothing to do now except return home to grieve and honor his memory. And so we told each other the story of what might have been and what had happened, the events fixed in our minds. It was a story we knew well, one of hope found then destroyed, of darkness overcoming light—of an earth too small to hold heaven. We'd lived this story before and knew the tale well. This time, though, seemed the worst of all. We'd waited so long, we'd believed that we'd finally found all we'd ever dreamed, that we'd never have to revisit grief again, not like this.*
>
> *As we walked, sinking ever deeper into hopelessness, a man approached us. "What's this you're discussing so intently and with such sadness?" he asked. So we began to tell him all that had happened. We told him of our frozen hopes and of dreams dashed. And we also confessed our confusion—the women had seen angels and heard them tell them he was alive. We had not.*
>
> *We left unspoken the questions that hammered at our hearts: Do we dare to believe? Do we dare to choose miracles?*

Choosing Miracles

"Every decision I make is a choice between a grievance and a miracle. I let go of grievances and choose miracles" (D. Chopra)

Once light is intentionally chosen, miracles emerge, daring us to believe in the illogical, unexpected and impossible. For me, this choice started with my intention to hear the story of my friendship differently and no longer see the present through the past. It continued with asking to see and returning love's gaze.

Hearing the Story Differently

The sense of heaven on earth I found as my friendship continued and deepened repeatedly challenged my old stories about how reality (and deep friendship) worked. For many years I'd walked about with grief in my heart. A story of disillusionment and loss repeatedly resurfaced when things seemed too good to be true as well as when they didn't seem as good as I wanted them to be. It was a story that questioned the reality of Infinite Light and Love as a real and palpable here and now. Where were they when I'd wanted them in the past? Where had they been when this or that happened? Why had God not answered my prayers?

As I reflected on these questions, I began to hear the story differently. It started after I'd read one writer's account of an Old Testament story.[22] Daniel, a faithful servant of God, had been mourning and praying to God without any discernible response for 21 days. On the 21st day an angel comes and says, "Daniel, don't be afraid. God has heard your prayer *ever since the first day*...I have come in answer to your prayer"(emphasis added).[23] This story opened my heart to the beginning of a vision of Infinite Light and Love different from the one that fueled my fear and challenged my hope. It opened my mind to my heart's intuition that "powerlessness is never an empirical fact,"[24] but only a limited vision of what is possible within which we have become trapped.

I suddenly realized that Infinite Light and Love <u>had</u> answered my desperate pleas…and were still answering…ever since that day over 60 years ago when my soul's song had faded and I lost my sense of heaven on earth. I realized that my experiences in fact told a story of Infinite Light and Love spoken across centuries, syllable by syllable.

The Answer, In Syllables

I'm starting to see it now
You <u>have</u> been uttering Your answer to my desperate plea
cried out so long ago as my world trembled and shattered.
Ever so carefully
Year after year,
Step by step
Friend to friend
I wanted it sooner
I wanted it whole, all at once
When it came in pieces,
the words seemed to lose their meaning,
drawled out too slowly,
one syllable forgotten before the next sounded.

I believed each syllable would be the answer
And despaired as it slipped away,
leaving only echoes
Only now
Touched by love long enough and deeply enough
to penetrate the silence between the syllables
I begin to recognize Your answer

There are some who say that recognition lies in the relationship between persons, rather than "out there" in objective reality. Perhaps it isn't until we allow visual data to connect with the image in our hearts that recognition actually occurs. Maybe that explains why I began to recognize the presence of heaven on earth more fully only as my heart opened. I started to perceive every disheartening event as a call to reconnect with light and miracles rather than as an invalidation of connection.

Allowing myself to listen for my heart's telling of my story returned me to my soul's song every time. Infinite Light and Love called me to hear it as a story of redemption and gift rather than of chaos without pattern or loss without redemption.

It was a story of hope unfolded across centuries, of dreams fulfilled, of success of an entirely different kind than I might have envisioned. Somewhere in another country, someone I'd never met had been born and come to write a book that was published at just the right time to come into my hands and turn me toward a long lost friend. Through radically different histories and families my friend and I had come to one time and space.

As I struggled to see what was before me at this point in my journey, I recognized the need to pay attention to my own heart and hear its story in place of the one I'd made up. I remembered the rest of the original Emmaus story. The man encountered on the road to Emmaus responds to the apostles' despair and disillusionment by telling Jesus' story differently, starting with the Old Testament prophets. I wrapped this story around my own and imagined myself on that same road to Emmaus.

<u>Scripture Meditation: Road to Emmaus (Part II)</u> *(Luke 24: 25-32)*

> *We finished telling this man who had joined us all that had happened. Our doubts, confusion and yearning to believe that all we had known wasn't lost must have been all too clear as we spoke. "Don't you remember?" he responded, and began to tell us the story as he heard it. He started it in a different place and added*

pieces we'd forgotten to include. As we listened, the ardor we'd thought we'd lost stirred within us once again. When we turned into the village, he gave us the impression he wouldn't be coming with us. We weren't ready to lose touch with what he'd reawakened within us. We were "hooked" into the story, into how he could see things entirely differently.

"Stay; don't leave," we said. " Come share our hearth and home." He did and there, as we broke bread in the warm intimacy of fire and friendship, our eyes opened to Love's undying presence. God had not abandoned us. Instead, undeterred by our illusions, Love still sought us out.

Love lived, undamaged in the face of the worst man could do, waiting only to be invited in. We realized that, if we were going to really believe, the imagined and assuredly terrible future we imagined and feared had to be released. Only then could we embrace the reality before us.[25] *We surrendered to the experience of re-found intimacy and turned back to Jerusalem.*

Asking to See

For more years then I want to admit I have kept revising map after map of my path as it resisted being placed in the neat boxes of my expectations and explanations. Finally, one day, I found that I could generate no more maps with which to disguise my blindness. My path challenged my homemade images of what heaven on earth should look like or where it would take me. Instead of smoothly unfolding in conformity with my expectations and dreams, the living and unpredictable spirit of Infinite Light and Love came before me, not to fulfill my wishes but to animate and bring to life the reality of a heaven-sized earth.

In response, I started to seek true sight. Bit by bit, I started to render to Infinite Light and Love more of the blindness I'd believed to be my vision. It was then that I found a translation of Our Father by Neil Douglas-Klotz. I would paraphrase the latter half of that translation as follows:

> *Give us today the sustenance of your love*
> *Release us from the knots into which we tie ourselves and others*
> *As we release them from the knots they've tied around us*
> *Keep us from inner agitation, doubt and fear*
> *For yours is the song that sounds from gathering to gathering.*
> *Amen*[26] *[emphasis added]*

As I meditated on different hearing and different seeing, I started to dare to return love's gaze without conditions. I remembered two stories about blindness and releasing knots. The first was about a rich young man who came to Jesus asking, "What can I do to achieve eternal life?" The second is about a very different man. This second man, Bartimeus—poor and a beggar—did not ask what he could do. Rather he cried out for mercy from a distance.

Jesus' response to each is similarly distinct. To the rich young man he says, "Sell all you possess and give to the poor." To the second he asks, "What do you want?" I imagined myself as a third person familiar with both men, knowing I carried them both within me.

Scripture Meditation: The Rich Young Man and Bartimeus *(Mark 10: 17-22; 46-52)*

I kept trying to make sense of Jesus' words and actions. I'm still trying. Just the other day I remembered the stories of these two men. I'd never thought of them together, but now I wonder if that wasn't what He meant us to do.

One man was young, secure in his material wealth and his ability to keep the law. His name was never recorded. The other man was Bartimeus, the son of Timmaaeus, blind and a beggar. He was not rich in material possessions. Time and circumstances had whittled away his sense of self-sufficiency.

I remembered that the rich young man had approached directly, walking right up to ask what he needed to do to attain eternal life. He didn't hesitate a second when you spoke of following the commandments, confidently answering that he already did all that. Yet he obviously wasn't yet happy because he asked one more time "What more do I lack?" His whole focus remained on what he needed to do. He looked somehow sad, though, when he asked that second question. He looked even sadder when you responded by telling him to go find out who he was beneath and beyond all he'd accumulated and accomplished, to enter into the mystery of love rather than the story of control and achievement.

He missed your point, I think. I know I did, until much later, after I'd met and gotten to know Bartimeus. Similar, yet so different. He also called out to You, feeling the need of something more. He didn't approach You directly, though, as did the young man. He only called out from a distance. Maybe, recognizing his own lack of sight, he didn't believe he could find his way to You on his own. Maybe he was afraid of coming to You only to be pushed away, found not good enough. Certainly that was the message from the people around him, "Shut up. Stop yelling. If He'd wanted to answer, He'd have done so already."

Did he really expect You to respond? I don't know. I wasn't sure myself as I waited to hear the rest of his story. He'd already been calling for quite a while before You told some of those with you to go get him. As soon as they did, he dropped the cloak that had hidden his face and jumped up, holding out his hands to be led to you. He stumbled a bit, not approaching erect and with confidence, but with his heart in his hands—out there in the open, no longer hidden by that thin and tattered cloak that had protected him for so long. It was as I heard that part that I finally understood. Bartimeus had gotten it. He'd asked to see, not to do. He'd realized that is wasn't up to him—that, ultimately, it wasn't about getting a map to follow, but about opening his eyes to the bellwether presence of Love Incarnate.

Love's Gaze Returned

The experience of returning love's gaze without conditions is beautifully captured in Madeleine L'Engle's poem *After Annunciation*:

"This is the irrational season,
when love blooms bright and wild.
Had Mary been filled with reason,
there'd been no room for the child."[27]

These words reflect an important aspect of returning love's gaze without conditions: an acceptance of absurdity that defies both logic and imagination.

Surprisingly, stepping outside my imagination turned out to be more difficult than surrendering my logic, perhaps because logic was a relative newcomer compared to the imagination I'd cherished and honed since childhood. Surrendering the boundaries of my imagination meant giving up the very tool that had helped me remember and hold on to that toward which my soul's song called me.

I wrote a meditation on the surrender of an imagined heaven, using a figure familiar to my childhood: Mary Magdalene. She, too, had struggled to return love's gaze without conditions as she faced a beloved whose presence defied both logic and imagination. The sentiments are familiar, I think, when we face what we deeply love, whether a person, a dream or something else.

The beginning:

I imagined such a world!
I created and nurtured it with my dreams
Sustained it with morsels of reality I found here
And there
People told me it was only make believe
And I could not refute that
But I held on
Then, one day, I met you
And the morsels became a banquet
I rejoiced
Here was the world I'd imagined
Not yet realized
Yet certainly here

The crucifixion:

Until that one day
When that other reality—the one I'd learned to fear—

Overshadowed the world I was only just beginning to believe could truly exist
as more than just a moment here and there
But even then I held on…
waiting,
it hurt too much to let go

The garden:
Suddenly, there you were
Returning my gaze
You stood before me
with me once more
I opened my arms
to embrace my dream come true
But not yet
"Don't cling to me," I heard
My heart broke
I stood paralyzed
at the edges of my imagination
seeing no world beyond it
only emptiness and darkness

The invitation:
I didn't hear the invitation in your voice—not then
The invitation to step beyond the world I'd created in my imagination
into the miracle of Love and Light unending
(No miracle can ever be fully imagined)
I hear it now

"Don't cling to me."
Stop trying to keep things as they were
Stop resisting what you cannot even imagine
Stop imagining them as you think they are now
not enough,
incomplete,
only morsels

Step outside the limits of your imagination
And join with me
Not as you've imagined
But as (and where) I live

It took only one step back
To move forward
And find myself
Where I'd always wanted to be
Beyond my wildest dreams!

I read and reread the story of Mary Magdalene coming to Jesus' tomb after he had been buried. Her encounter with Jesus resurrected fascinated me. The longed for reunion it depicted stirred a deep yearning within me even as Jesus' words to her not to cling unsettled me, feeling like an all too familiar rejection.

I imagined what Mary might have been thinking and feeling.

<u>Scripture Meditation: Mary Magdalene</u> *(John 20:16-17)*

> *I heard him call my name and knew that I was loved more deeply than I could even imagine. I turned with open arms. I wanted so much to touch him, to feel his arms around me just one more time. I'd envied Thomas that when I heard of his embrace. I, too, needed physical reassurance. Not so much reassurance that my Beloved was really there, but rather reassurance that I'd always be able to be with him, that I'd always have his palpable touch. Yet, as I turned toward him, he told me not to come near. I just looked at him, not understanding, tears in my eyes. I was barely able to contain the deep grief welling up in me. And I realized that I still grieve the loss of that touch all these years,*

even as my faith in our connection deepens. I thought it was an ending.

As I imagined this scene I knew that I remained both doubter and believer, still seeking proof and reassurance, still struggling between surrendering and holding, still believing yet not fully believing. I am only now beginning to understand it was a beginning.

Harvesting the Wonders:

FAIRYTALE COME TRUE

"This is how haloes are seen, by looking up into largeness, by tucking smallness into the field of infinity." (J. Shea)

Infinite Light and Love became increasingly palpable as my friendship continued. After a divorce and years when all my experience seemed to only confirm I'd never find the love for which I yearned, I felt a fairytale had come true. The wider spiritual landscape that had been friendship's implicit background became explicit foreground: anchor, context, and substance. Love, light, and miracles became not just "...belief or possibility but certainty and reality."[28] Their relational and incarnational aspects, which I'd struggled to hold, now started to hold me. Words I found on a Hallmark product echoed how I felt: "Once in a while, in the middle of an ordinary life, love gives us a fairytale." (No source given)

The words of another writer resonated for me: "In all people, in all places, in every created thing the light of God's creation is shining. It may be buried and forgotten under layers of darkness and distortion but it is there waiting to be discovered."[29] As I realized the depth and constancy of the friendship offered me, I began to delight in Infinite Light and Love

> "everywhere...
> in the turning of a corner
> in the eyes
> and on the lips
> of a stranger [and a friend],
> [even] in the emptiest areas
> where is no place for hope...
> incomprehensible
> inexplicable..." [30]

I realized that my task and challenge now was to harvest the energy of Infinite Light and Love: to both allow its energy "to drive deep into [me]," and *simultaneously* allow my "yearning, outstretched hands...to pierce the heart of God" and bring it forth to be unveiled into form (emphasis added),[31] its wonders "expressed in[to] the dimension of the sensible."[32] I began to reflect on three dimensions of that expression: priceless treasure, incredible truths, and transformation.

Priceless Treasures

The most priceless treasures are not always the most easily recognized.

Every fairytale is in some way about a journey to obtain a priceless treasure. Whatever its form, obtaining this treasure lies at the core of every tale's "happily ever after." My journey was initiated and sustained by my desire for the treasure of heaven on earth, whose reality I could once more remember echoing through my soul's song. I reflected on the priceless treasures offered me through the metaphors of a field that contained a hidden treasure, a pearl, and a tiny mustard seed.

A Field

Though composed of many ordinary experiences, the "field" of Light and Love that surrounded my deep friendship and within which it existed was extraordinary.

It was, in a way, the love between my friend and I, with God as its owner. It was also the love within me, which I needed to acknowledge and return to its proper source before its full treasure could be unearthed into the light. It was, of course, both and more. The ground on which I walked was the realm of Incarnate Love, in which my deep friendship lived and moved and had its being.

I remembered a story about a field and imagined myself walking home one day, perhaps like the man in the story.

Scripture Meditation: Treasure Buried in a Field (Matthew 13:44)

I'd taken a different route than my usual, one I hadn't taken in a long time. I'd forgotten how beautiful and restful it was. There was a brook and all these wild flowers blooming like a multi-colored carpet underneath the trees. I stopped to breathe it all in. I wanted to always be able to see the flowers, to hear the water as it tumbled over rocks or lay in still pools, mirroring sky and color. It must be for sale, I thought to myself, and decided to purchase it. It seemed like a simple thing to do. Little did I know then that it was to become both my greatest challenge and deepest joy.

I set off to find the owner only to discover that it was not an easy task. Time passed as I searched and the flowers faded into winter's brown. The brook that had flowed noisily through the field slowed and didn't seem to make as much music. Even so, I kept seeking, remembering my soul's response to the colors and the sounds, unwilling to forget the warm breeze that had caressed my heart with tenderness beyond words. More time passed, and when I'd almost given up hope, the colors and sounds returned. I learned that they had never gone away but had only been in hibernation, hidden by season's change.

One day after that, I did find the owner and offered to purchase the field. "The price is quite high," he responded. "Whatever it costs," I answered, though I didn't really know just what I'd agreed to. What I had come to know, however, was that there are fields worth much more than can be counted.

A Pearl

We tend to believe that "miracles only take moments of intensity." The truth though is that miracles "take time—and all you've got to give." [33] In this way they are somewhat like pearls, I think. Oysters form pearls slowly, layer by layer. Buried deeply in the oyster's very flesh they remain hidden. They are not easily obtained. Divers must suspend their reliance on surface light and air to go into the deep to obtain them.

I reflected on how the gift of friendship returned to me could be likened to a pearl. It too took time and all I had to give. Much of it remained hidden, buried in my heart. Like a pearl diver, I, too, often needed to suspend my reliance on surface light and air to go into the deep.

There is a scripture story about a "a jewel merchant on the hunt."[34] For many years I'd believed the story to be about just the pearl for which the merchant hunted. As my journey continued, though, I started to question whether the story was not in fact about more. Perhaps it was instead a story about the passionate desire that inspired the hunt. Perhaps the pearl's value was based on something beyond flawless beauty, something that could be seen only with practice and perseverance born of deep desire, like those magical images that looked at in just the right way become 3-dimensional and reveal a deeper image.

I imagined myself a seeker like that merchant in that story.

<u>Scripture Meditation: Pearl Without Price (Matthew 13:46)</u>

> *I had looked for so long for just the right pearl. I wasn't even sure what would make it the right one. I did remember I'd seen it once when I was much younger. It was then that, without really knowing it, I'd fallen in love with it. But I'd gone looking for other treasures, not realizing its true value. Then one day there it*

was, even more beautiful then I remembered. All I'd amassed paled in comparison. I looked into its depths and saw all I'd been seeking and trying to purchase for so long. My heart opened, releasing all I'd held as mine. I knew now that what I needed to give to receive its beauty was not a price paid. It was gift given in response to gift, all I had, my very self. I received it, not as one more possession but as unearned precious gift.

A Tiny Seed

It was a tiny seed in the beginning, this deep friendship unexpectedly returned to me. I did not recognize its value at first; it gave no hint of its potential to lead me into heaven on earth. Only as I allowed it to sink into my heart's soil did its full value begin to be apparent. Even then, though, it was not quite as I'd expected.

It didn't grow like a beautiful flower. It grew more like a weed: in its own way, independent of any efforts to tame or cultivate it. It challenged me to acknowledge the value of those dimensions of friendship that also grow wild and can be neither tamed nor cultivated. It invited me to see the strength of those dimensions, their offer of shade and shelter. It took a while for me to learn that weeds—those aspects of my friendship that I found frustrating and could not control—were merely flowers that refused to fit into my predefined boxes of what deep friendship should look like or be like.

I'd heard a scripture story about heaven on earth that told how it, too, grew from a tiny seed of a weed, which when planted unfolded its wild potential and grew larger than all other carefully cultivated plants. I searched for that story and imagined myself as the sower.

Scripture Meditation: A Mustard Seed (Matthew 13:31)

> *I pondered the mystery of that tiny mustard seed sowed so long ago. Friends and neighbors must have thought I'd lost my mind. It was, after all, only a weed. "It'll grow wild, you know, you won't be able to control it" some said. "You can't use it for anything," others added. Yet, though I wasn't sure why, I knew I needed to care for it and so I did. Now, it was full-grown. A multitude of birds nested in its branches, twittering their cheerful song. I'd come to cherish this wild plant: its independence, its drive to flourish even in the driest of times, its generous offering of shade and shelter. I remembered the story that likened it to heaven on earth. I walked over to sit beneath its branches. There was still so much for it to teach me.*

Incredible Truths

"Alice laughed. 'There's no use trying,' she said.
'One can't believe impossible things.'
"I daresay you haven't had much practice,' said the Queen. 'When I was your age, I always did it for half-an-hour a day. Why, sometimes I've believed as many as six impossible things before breakfast." (Carroll, 1999)

How easily we believe we can infallibly determine what is possible and what is not. Fairytales challenge that belief. They present us with seemingly impossible realities that bend the laws of science along with our assumptions about reality. My continuing friendship with my beloved friend—and the heaven on earth it unveiled for me—was like a fairytale in that sense: something I'd never believed possible, an incredible truth.

The Immensity of Unearned Love

The persistent belief that love must be somehow earned or at least paid for was often at the center of my making believe. It undermined my deeper believing. I didn't know—or imagine— that I could receive all I'd ever wanted if only I could let go of what I clung to so persistently.

There is story told about a man who loved his homeland of Crete passionately.[35] Indeed, what he feared most about dying was leaving Crete. So, as he sensed that death was near, he placed a few grains of Crete's soil in his hand and told his family to bury him with them. After he died, the story continues, he found himself at heaven's gate with the soil still in his hand. As he tried to enter, however, he discovered that the gate was locked. Not knowing what to do, he waited. After a while, St. Peter came out to see him and told him that he could not come in until he released that bit of soil. The man replied that he could not do so. "…it's all that I know and love, it's Crete! I will not let it go."[36] On hearing this, St. Peter went back through the gate and left him alone outside.

A short while later, the gates unexpectedly reopened and a little girl came out. "She did not try to reason with him, nor did she try to coax him into letting go of the soil. She simply took his hand and, as she did, the soil of Crete spilled to the ground. Then she led him through the gates of heaven where to his total amazement he found that "there before him lay all of Crete."[37]

Like the man in the story I had difficulty believing the immensity of unearned love offered to me, thinking instead that I needed to earn and cling to what love I experienced. Perhaps it was because I believed I was unworthy to be loved, or perhaps it was that in insisting that love must be earned I could hold on to my illusion of control. When things did not work out as I wanted, I could tell myself that I hadn't done the right thing or set the right conditions. If I would only do this, or that, I thought, everything will work out.

For a long time (and still sometimes) I repeatedly examined my actions and those of my friend, trying to find the key to preserving the aspects of our friendship I most desired. I could think of so many instances that seemed to violate the truth of unearned love…or was it me who violated it?

As I reflected further, I was reminded that neither the concrete experiences of God's love reflected in others' response to me, nor the heaven on earth these opened were of my creation. They were true gifts. While certainly beyond all I could deduce or comprehend, they were nevertheless simultaneously consonant with my own deepest self—that was the hard part to trust.

The story of the lilies of the field tells of unconditional and wholehearted gifts, of Infinite Light and Love that works with and for us. I remembered a parable you told once, Beloved. It was about the lilies of the field who neither toiled nor spun yet were clothed in glory. I imagined myself hearing that story and reflecting on its meaning for me.

Scripture Meditation: Lilies of the field (Luke 12:27)

> *Unlike the lilies in your story, I've so often fixed my attention on clothing myself with garments of my own making, blind to what is so freely given—or thinking it's not for me. I focus on my efforts instead of the gifts before me. It's like when I'm in the water, trying to swim. I tend to believe that I can stay afloat only through my own effort. I forget about the water's nature, without which I could never remain afloat no matter how hard I worked. It is difficult to trust as radically as do the lilies. And yet, if I listen very, very carefully to the notes of my soul's song I hear the truth of an immense, unconditional and unearned love within which there was no separation between giver and given.*

The Power of a Trusting Voice

Stories about the immensity of unearned love insist that love is never the outcome of what we do. It is neither earned nor purchased. There are, however, also contrasting stories that tell about asking for what we want. These add a second incredible dimension to love's dynamics. They tell us there is so much more to love than remaining only passive recipients of its unearned gifts.

I've struggled to integrate both dimensions. At times I've emphasized my power to shape and control. At other times I've found myself sinking into a sense of powerlessness. My tendency has been to make it either all about one or the other. Caught in this seemingly irreconcilable contradiction I disallow the promise and potential of paradox—the amazing truth of two apparently contradictory things that are both true at the same time.

Only as my experience of friendship deepened did I find myself plumbing the depths of love's paradox. I realized I needed to conceive of its power differently from how I'd conceived of it for so long. I read and reread your words in scripture about receiving. I imagined I was there to hear you, Beloved, speak and could walk up to talk with you.

Scripture Meditation: Knock and It Will Open (Luke 11:9-12)

> *You asked us to surrender to Divine will and, at the same time, promised that we would find if we only asked. Up until now, I've alternated my attention between these two messages rather than looking at them simultaneously. I am only now beginning to understand. You ask us to neither lie inert letting the current take us where it will nor to assume that it is only our own efforts that takes us where we go. Our attention to and reliance on the current is as necessary as our own movements. I have heard one version of*

your saying: "when you ask in my Father's name." Perhaps that is the key: asking as one asks someone loved deeply, with humility ("it's not all about me") and respect ("you are equally competent and caring"), while at the same time trusting that our desire is received with humility and respect as well—a thought even more radical than the first.

Deep friendship is grounded in reciprocal relationship. God is both astonishingly humble and immeasurably respectful, believing in our ability to love, repeatedly putting faith in us to respond, giving us free will while simultaneously offering us all. That was the part I'd been missing all this time.

The Strength of Sustained Readiness

I explored and experimented with the paradox of trusting surrender and hopeful asking. Hoping for, rather than trying to force, what I wanted in my friendship or how I wanted it was not easy. My tendency was to either not hope at all—and call myself foolish for thinking that I could hope—or to hope wildly and then, when things did not happen when or how I wanted, use that as evidence of hope's futility. Slowly, my friend's steadfast presence invited me to both wait with deep hope and act with enduring faith no matter what.

I was drawn to reflect on a scripture story of sustained readiness. It tells of laborers waiting to be hired. I imagined being there, like the men in the story.

<u>Scripture Meditation: Waiting (Matthew 20:8-16)</u>

I had been waiting almost all day to be hired. Each time they came to hire my spirit would lift and I would try to get their attention. And each time as they chose others then went away, leaving me behind, my spirit fell. As the day wore on, others who waited with me started to go home. "At least we can do something there," they'd say. "Here all we are doing is wasting time. It's no use hoping. Even if we are hired, it is late in the day and we will earn so little that it will not be worth it."

But I stayed; I could not bear to leave. There were a few others who stayed with me. We refused to give up. Just last week we had heard that new teacher in town. He has said to ask and we would be given. We decided to believe him and wait in hope rather than fixed expectation. It wasn't easy. My expectations rose every time a new employer came again, only to ebb as they left without choosing me.

And then, almost at the end of the afternoon someone came. This last person looked directly at me and at the others as he said, "Come, you are still wanted." We jumped up and went without a second thought, our hope renewed.

At the vineyard we worked as hard as all the others, even though we knew we would earn less. A tiny spark of persistent hope, of prayers answered, refused to fade. At the end of the day we were called up first when it was time to get paid. To our total shock, we received a full day's wages! It was unbelievable. It was a lesson about the dynamics of effort and gift that I'll never forget. Perhaps it was then that my transformation truly started.

Transformation

"When a man or a woman undergoes a deep spiritual transformation, there are certain critical points along the way when what is partial needs to be shattered in order to become whole." (S. Mitchell)

Transformation is a common element of fairytales: frogs turn into prices,[38] ugly ducklings transform into swans, sleeping beauties awaken from their comas, weaklings turn into heroes. As my journey through deep friendship's inner spiritual landscape continued, I started to realize that in their own way these stories echoed the transformation triggered within me. True heaven on earth transformations, however, are almost always slower and messier than those described in fairytales.

A friend once gave me a card that read "God gives us dreams a size too big so that we can grow into them." Deep friendship is like that, I think, given to us "a size too big." It can be tempting to alter circumstances to fit. I tried that for a while. Thankfully, my friend remained steadfast Thankfully also, friendship's priceless treasures and incredible truths refused to shrink to my self-imagined dimensions. They—and my beloved friend—kept challenging me to expand rather than shrink my heart and vision.

Led by Love

Several years passed since I'd first reconnected with my friend. I'd come so far, through times of wonder as well as times of doubt and confusion. Then, with no warning, it all started to feel like I'd only been going around in circles, led by illusions of love rather than by love. It all somehow felt more like holding on to a photographic negative than a real image. Subtly, without awareness, as my friendship seemed to stall, I had allowed my fear to become more important than my love. Only when I once more made love more important than my fear did I begin to be transformed.

I found a scripture story about such a transformation. I pictured the scene and imagined myself as a witness to what happened.

Scripture Meditation: The Wedding Feast (John 2:3)

> *I'll remember that wedding feast, when water was turned into wine. Those of us who were there still talk about all we experienced and learned that day. Like the water turned into wine, we were all transformed as we participated in what happened. For me, though, it has been what I've learned since then that has transformed me most deeply. Your first response was to say that it wasn't your time. I've learned that love often speaks to us at unexpected times and makes unexpected requests—and that it is important at those times to shift our attention away from fear and follow the rhythm of love's timing rather than our own. You did that. You were willing to step beyond your own timing and act, though it wasn't your "turn." I'm still working on that one. Some days my spirit is transformed like water into wine. Other days it seems like nothing changes. But I still remember and believe.*

Committed to Faithful Response

A recurrent theme in fairytales is the commitment to respond with deep faith no matter how different things may seem from what is envisioned or desired. Beauty must return to her Beast, the Princess must kiss her frog. Only then, it seems, can a fuller reality reveal itself. The lesson seems to be that the deepest transformations follow rather than precede commitment to an action. One writer echoes this point succinctly when he points out the "intentional inversion of *do* and *hear*—commitment and discernment..."[39] affirmed in Exodus 24:7: "All that the Lord has said shall we do then hear." This same inversion is echoed in the story told of Nachson, a Jewish man who though not knowing how to swim must jump into the Red Sea before it will part.[40]

When I could hear love's voice, opening my spirit sufficiently to commit to faithful response—to do—was not hard. When I could not, however, when I needed to act first, it was all too easy to question and doubt the direction of my journey. My perceptions and certainty of deep friendship's treasures and truths were harder to hold on to when I experienced a reality disparate from that I envisioned and yearned for.

Boehme, a 17th century mystic, presents a metaphor of two eyes, one that looks out at the sensory, physical world and one whose gaze is fixed on heaven, the realm within and beyond that world. [41] Only when we stand faithful, he says, can these eyes remain connected, joining the two worlds into one. When not connected, our vision shatters, allowing images and sounds of fear to emerge. "The voice of love says God is with you, you can endure [and even soar like an eagle]. The voice of fear says give up, run away...distance yourself emotionally from the person or thing you think is causing you pain."[42] For me, there came a time when I realized that my commitment to respond in accordance with love's voice, which was always constant though not always audible, needed to precede my perception of its presence, which was never constant.

As I found myself in places that tested my commitment to faithful action, it was tempting to become mired in the questions posed by fear: How would I survive? How could I move past the places that didn't match my vision? How could I avoid or master them? How could I know for sure that it was all really true? Slowly I learned the one response that consistently transformed those places from trial to gift and my experience of them from struggle to dance: "Yes." [43]

Until I said "Yes, here is where love has led me; Yes, here is where its voice seeks to be sung," nothing changed. With each "yes," though, my vision of where I stood and what was before me became clearer. Each "yes" realigned my song with the truths and treasures of heaven so that love's presence was once more a palpable experience beyond any fear or question triggered by external manifestations.

I remembered a story of the time Jesus wandered in the desert for forty days. There, he, too, heard other voices challenging his commitment to faithful response. I imagined hearing the story;. I reflected on how I might have responded had it happened to me.

Scripture Meditation: Tempted by Other Voices (Matthew 4:1-11)

> *At first, there was no question that in the face of such temptations I, too, would have stood firm; I was so sure of myself. Only as time went on and my confidence eroded did I begin to find a deeper meaning in your words. It was as I experienced the stark contrast between my own experiences of hunger, weakness and yearning and the heaven on earth I envisioned that I began to really understand your story and its message.*
>
> *Like a butterfly asked to stop flying, the price of choosing fear over love became more and more unbearable. I realized that power severed from love can impose connection but can never live connection. On its own, such power can only act on the world, and to do that it must first tear heaven and earth apart. Ultimately, it was only repeated reaffirming of my commitment to faithful action (i.e., lived connection) that gave me the strength to turn away from the voices that urged me to first hear them and then act. Commitment to faithful action always transformed hunger into nourishment, weakness into strength, and yearning into fulfillment.*

Open to Spirit

As I write this reflection I am aware that its greatest challenge lies not in embracing spirit but rather in letting Spirit embrace me. Yet, when Spirit asked me let it come into my heart no matter its condition, I felt it was somewhat like allowing someone into my house: OK when I've cleaned and organized and prepared but not OK before it's clean enough or organized enough.

Spirit, though, asked me let it come into my heart no matter its condition. When I did that, I found myself taken to the hidden edges of my being. There, the limits of self-imposed boundaries etched by the desires and visions I held so closely to my heart were laid bare. I feared that these boundaries, like a house not yet ready to be seen, would be judged and found wanting—how could they not? Yet, houses with doors that are not opened until we deem them ready remain forever waiting to be entered.

Spirit's territory, while often resonant with my own spirit, nevertheless lay outside my self-imposed boundaries. It called me to discover what was beyond my vision, even when I believed my vision held all I'd ever want. Following love's call and remaining committed to faithful response were acts of my own will. Opening to Spirit, however, was not. It required going beyond the narrow constraints of my will even when I feared that moving beyond those constraints meant only certain loss. Old questions reawakened. Will Spirit's currents hold me? Will I fly? I sought assurance to quiet fear's voice, which conveniently forgot to say that there is no assurance in staying on firm ground either, only its illusion. At the same time, love's voice quietly insisted that to receive the assurance I so deeply yearned for, I needed to let myself be embraced and carried by Spirit.

Gradually, transformation became means rather than outcome. As one writer puts it: "It is in the act of offering our hearts in faith that something in us transforms, and what may have been merely a remote abstraction flames into life."[44] I remembered a story about

Jesus asking Peter to open to spirit and imagined myself as Peter's companion that day.

Scripture Meditation: Pushing Back into Deep Water (Luke5: 8, 10)

> *I'd been out with Peter that day and night, searching for what would feed us. Bone-weary and heart-tired, with nothing to show for all our efforts. I turned with him toward familiar shores. You were there, as we were pulling in. And you asked us to push back into deep water. I could see neither reason nor sense to it, but I did it, because you asked. And then it happened, abundance beyond measure, surpassing my understanding or grasp. In an instant I realized how closed I'd been, how little of God's being I'd allowed into my own. Your earlier words about needing to be born of spirit echoed in my mind. I began to understand that following you and remaining committed to your truths were not enough. They could lead me back into the deep, even to the threshold of heaven. They could change me. But they could not transform me. That part was not mine to do, only to receive. I opened my heart once more to walk this landscape of deep friendship with Infinite Light and Love.*

Unmapped Believing:

JOB'S DILEMMA[45]

"En la noche dichosa, en secreto, que nadie me veía ni yo miraba cosa, sin otra luz o guía sino la que en mi corazón ardía" **(St. John of the Cross)**
On that wondrous night, in secret, when no one saw me nor I saw any thing, with no other light or guide than that which in my heart burned. (personal translation)

Sometime after the first year or so after my friend and I had reconnected, there came a time when, as so often happens in close friendships, I became more aware of what was not going as I wished than of what remained steadfast and true. My friend and I talked with less regularity. Disagreements erupted and disrupted the wondrous harmony we'd experienced before. One or the other of us would do or say something that was received with less than delight by the other. Most devastating of all to me, my friend told me that marriage was not an option.

I didn't want to lose my friend's love, yet I began to wonder if we were meant to stay connected at all. Was all of this a sign that our friendship was not meant to be any longer? It seemed to fade, even disappear at times, as did my own feelings for him. It all seemed to be coming to an end and I found myself in the dark, with no map to guide me and no light except that which refused to go out in my heart. I searched for others' stories in the belief that "the value of another's experience is to give us hope, [rather than] to tell us how to proceed."[46]

Slowly time and trust led me to recognize the absence of familiar maps as an integral albeit paradoxical part of love's gift. As one writer put it, "Silence is the friend who challenges us to be healed when we simply wish to be soothed."[47] I came to recognize that with apparent darkness came the courage to move beyond my safe spaces, to where both my greatest gifts and God's deepest presence were to be found. I realized that, up until now, I'd largely been focused on getting to a specific destination as I'd envisioned it. I started to wonder if perhaps I shouldn't instead be focused on learning love's path so intimately that I could travel it even when its only light and guidance came from my soul song's burning in my heart.

It wasn't that all had been clear up until now. When I'd ended up in unmapped territory before, though, I'd simply focused on studying the maps I'd drawn more carefully or on extending them into new territory. Now, I was beginning to suspect that the territory in which I found myself was ultimately unmappable. It was, in fact, territory that could not be mapped without distorting its reality as well as the reality of the love that led me into it. Echoes of words I'd once read came back, reminding me that "our uncertainty is necessary and holy. If we dispel it, we cannot avoid destroying mystery also—the very thing we seek. Mystery cannot be cut down to human [map-able] size. It cannot be made comprehensible...."[48]

Staying true to the path deep friendship called me into brought me into necessary and holy uncertainty. Loving my friend—and remaining receptive to his love—meant loving even when he responded in ways that made no sense to me.[49] I know that there were times I responded in ways that made no sense to him.

I was reminded of Job's story in the Old Testament. I started to see it as a story not about overcoming adversity but about how to live loving—and being loved—when circumstances contradict the very maps created to hold that loving.

As things seemed to become more and more senseless, Job could not make sense of (i.e., had no map for) what was happening. Though my experience was not as devastating as Job's, I found myself at such a time now, a time when how I believed God (and my friend) would and should act seemed to have no link with what was actually happening. In the past, at times like these, I'd tried to change my friend or failing that, God. Neither of those options proved sufficient now. My only viable option was to remain in the tension of uncertainty and allow my commitment to friendship's path to stand on nothing but love itself.

Job's friends tried to help by offering answers ("maps") of various sorts. Job, however, refused to step into those maps at the expense of his lived relationship with God. He refused to "earth-size" the mystery of infinite Love and Light. Perhaps he intuited, as I did, that doing so sacrifices the majesty of that reality. Job chose instead to remain steadfast, stripped of all that had defined him and his life up to that point, until earth (i.e., finite love and light) itself opened to embrace Infinite Light and Love (i.e., became heaven-sized).

The more I reflected on this aspect of Job's story, the more I came to understand the challenge of unmapped believing. It was not so much about releasing my attempts to understand WHY as about surrendering my attempts to figure out HOW: "*How* do [I] do it?" "*How* long will it take?" *How* much does it cost?" "*How* do [I] get [this]… situation to change?" "*How* do [I] measure [map] it?" "*How* can this be happening?"[50]

Gradually, I started to believe that the answers did not lie, as I once believed, in thinking that God wished to teach us a lesson or worse, take away all I held dear. Rather, I began to believe these times happen because only the depth of the unwavering commitment they stimulate can ensure that heaven (Infinite Light and Love) and earth (all we hold dear) remain one *no matter what*. They are the definitive answer to our prayers to be healed, though they may cause us to echo St. Teresa of Avila's words to God: "If this is how you treat your friends it's no wonder you have so few of them!"[51]

As I stood at the still-point of this dilemma, I realized that what I needed now was willingness to remain in mystery with questions to which I knew there might be no answer. I understood that this had in fact been God's challenge to Job: Can you answer the unanswerable; i.e., "Do you know where Light comes from and where Darkness lives? … And who do you think is the father of the rain and dew?" (Job 38: 18, 28). God was not saying, as I'd previously thought, "I know better, Job, so stop questioning."

Facing the challenge of believing "off the map" I started to hear something entirely different: "Look at who I (Infinite Light and Love) am. See me mirrored in the mystery of things greater and grander than you can understand. Don't judge me by the little things you can understand (and control). Wait. Trust. Let Infinite Light and Love in. More than you know or can imagine is not only possible, it is assured." Job wasn't getting an answer to quiet his questions; he was instead getting a response from within a space that precluded answers yet nevertheless held all Job sought.

I found inspiration in reading *The Answer to How Is Yes*, which interestingly is neither spiritual nor theological. There I read:

"*Yes* expresses our willingness to … discover the real meaning of commitment, which is to say *Yes* to causes that have no clear offer of a return, to say *Yes* when we do not have mastery or the methodology [i.e., map] to know how to get to where we want to go."[52] As I walked without a comprehensible map or route, guided only by the light shed by heaven's flame and sung by my heart, I discovered my ability to say "Yes" to mystery and found that was always, somehow, enough.

When I found myself in unmapped and unmappable territory, willing to release all my knowing in favor of coming face-to-face and heart-to-heart with mystery, that mystery itself revealed the presence and shape of Infinite Light and Love present in my life. In that Light and Love wonders greater than those I could imagine or comprehend manifested. Once again I found words that mirrored this reality: "A genuine path opens up before us, not in the direction of greater control [i.e., clearer maps] but toward greater intimacy. It releases us into learning to live within great unknowing…"[53] Gradually, I realized that "Yes" was sufficient response to the dilemma of walking the unmapped and unmappable territory. "Let us say Yes, again and again and again, and Yes some more."[54]

Halfway to the Miracle

"Love will serve no wine before its time." (M. Ryan)

As I struggled with the challenge of continuing to walk unmapped territory in the absence of the signposts I wanted, I ran across the phrase "halfway to the miracle."[55] This phrase instantly resonated with my feelings and became a central metaphor for my reflections. The miracle initiated by the renewed sounding of my soul's song remained incomplete as I found myself grappling with the experience of being stalled, stuck somewhere between where I'd started and where I so deeply desired to be. I'd found the heaven on earth my soul sang of and it had found me. Yet, now it seemed I could move no further. As I read "halfway to the miracle," it was the "halfway" part that grabbed my attention.

Like the proverbial half-empty/half-full glass, "halfway" could be read in two very different ways. It could be read to mean either "not there yet" or "almost there." I suddenly understood that focusing on being only halfway (i.e. not there yet) was like focusing only on the sliver of a new moon while remaining blind to the full of the moon outlined in the darkness behind it. The sliver is a partial illumination of a complete whole already present. The fullness is there (for there would be no sliver without it), just not yet fully illuminated.

As I learned to stay present rather than to flee into images of what could be but was not yet, something shifted. I started to perceive what already was not as an isolated and incomplete piece but as the foreground of an as yet unrevealed whole, something akin to dawn's light, generated from and sustained by an unseen source from which it cannot be separated. I surrendered my tight focus on the incompleteness of what was and turned my attention to more clearly perceiving and receiving the whole in which it nested. As I did, I realized more and more that the miracle of Infinite Light and Love I sought was not mine to create. It was mine only to allow and cultivate.

My sense of halfway shifted accordingly. I began to see the whole of the miracle I sought, outlined dark against dark, behind the brightly lit moments I cherished (my "slivers of the moon"). The entire miracle—God's dream of and for me and my friend—already was, fully present, just not yet fully unfolded into light. Like walking out into the night without a flashlight, it took a while for my sight to adjust. Slowly, though, I developed night vision and started to see by a softer, subtler light. This was the gift of being stalled "halfway:" time enough to realize that the miracle of Light and Love, as I'd imagined and expected it to manifest in my life, was only a "sliver" of the real thing.

Keep Believing

I still wondered at times if perhaps I needed to turn toward another path. Each time I'd regain confidence that I was on the right path, the signs of progress I'd expected would disappear and I'd find myself at the place of doubt all over again. I realized just how much I did not yet believe and how much I still focused on where I was not rather than on where I was. Like a child insistently asking "Are we there yet?" my "there" remained somewhere just out of reach.

Yet my soul's song remained insistent, reminding me that what I could see and experience was only one small part of the full miracle. It invited me to keep believing in and opening into a deeper intimacy with Infinite Love and Light. I began to understand that, like an infant waiting to be born, I was being held and "grown" until I could believe steadfastly enough to receive more than I dared imagine could really be.

I turned then to look for scripture stories about sustained believing. One such story was Jairus' story, which resonated with my use of the phrase "halfway to the miracle." It was not hard to picture myself as Jairus as he approached Jesus.

Scripture Meditation: Jairus *(Luke 8:41-49)*

> *There I was, the answer to my prayers within reach. I'd known just where to go and what to do: get to Jesus, ask for his healing, get the miracle. After all, he had said, "Knock and it shall be answered." It didn't quite go that way, though, or at least not as I'd understood those words. In fact, after I asked for healing for my daughter everything came to a stop, the response to my petition apparently derailed.*
>
> *I found myself off my carefully drawn map, without answers, stalled halfway to the miracle I so desperately desired. Jesus turned his attention to someone else. I didn't know what to do. To go back without his*

> *healing of my daughter was inconceivable. To push forward—to tell Jesus not to attend to this woman—was equally unacceptable. All I could do was shut my eyes and wait, almost afraid to breathe. And it was in the waiting that the true miracle unfolded. I had gone to seek healing for my daughter and found it for myself. In those few moments I realized my blindness and went home to find my daughter well.*

Just Say the Word

My sense that I was being held and grown by Infinite Light and Love amid and through the detours and commas to my journey steadily strengthened. I started to perceive both detours and commas more as expressions of an underlying rhythm and power rather than as disruptions or endings. I realized more surely that what I could see and experience directly was only one small part of the bigger, deeper and benign energy of Infinite Light and Love. It was not my thoughts or my words but the expression of that energy, its "word," that carried the miracle whose melody resonated in my soul's song. Once again, I faced the call to trust in the power of that word as I had trusted in the power of my own for so long.

I re-read a scripture story about a centurion, a man much like Jairus, whose understanding seemed to already have shifted from "part" to "whole." He seemed to have a faith I had yet to acquire. I wondered, had he too had many "halfways" in his life? How had he learned that, once spoken, words can carry a reality not yet evident? I imagined hearing his story once again.

Scripture Meditation: The Centurion *(Matthew 8:5-9):*

> *As I heard the centurion's story told and retold, I started to grasp the distinction between authority*

rooted in control (power over) and authority rooted in relationship (power with). The centurion trusted authority. Being a "man under authority," he had, I'm sure, both given and taken orders. He had come to trust the power of authority: an order given meant an order carried out. He trusted Jesus' authority as he trusted his own. I, too, have known the power of authority, I thought. Ironically though, it has led me to fear rather than to trust. To believe in the power of authority is one thing; to trust in its capacity to act on my behalf is another.

The centurion knew all about authority. He spoke in terms of commands given. Jesus knew about power rooted in love. He spoke in terms of love expressed. Commands can be trusted to initiate change. Only love can be trusted to heal.

Without Knowing the Day or the Hour

Though I was learning to accept detours and apparent stalls as well as to trust in the power of Light and Love to heal all that had deadened my spirit, I still found it so difficult not to know when or how.[56] I kept focusing on my frustration with feeling halfway rather than on the promise and gift of the underlying miracle: Infinite Light and Love unfolding on earth. There was, I slowly realized, yet a third thing I needed to meet the challenge of being halfway to the miracle: acceptance that the promise and gift of my journey would be realized even if I knew neither the day nor the hour.

Somehow my mind's knowing, whose timing was within my control, seemed so much more real than my heart's believing, which simply burst forth on its own schedule. I was like a reverse Mr. Magoo. Mr. Magoo, a terribly nearsighted cartoon character from the 1950's and 60's, walked untouched amid disaster after disaster without seeing any of them. I walked amid miracles with my attention elsewhere, all the time wondering when and how they would appear. Awake only to my dreams, I remained unaware of their realization.

It is said that there are Bushmen who are trained from an early age to heed the "tapping of their heart, [a] "mysterious kind of inner knowing"[57] that, if they remain attentive, will lead them to the truth of what is around them. In this way, they access the illumination necessary to sense what was coming and move accordingly without needing to know neither the day nor the hour.

One particular scripture story about delays and needing to stay alert kept coming to mind as I journeyed on. I had always interpreted this story to be about being prepared as I understood preparation: a gathering of needed supplies (i.e., self-reliance). I was beginning to understand it now as about surrender into love, a celebration of Infinite Light and Love.[58] I imagined myself telling Jesus of my new understanding.

<u>Scripture Meditation: Wise and Foolish Virgins (Matthew 25: 1-13):</u>

> *Like many others, I didn't understand this story about the wise and foolish virgins when you first told it. It seemed so simple. You wanted to be sure we gathered sufficient supplies to await your coming. Yet, that meaning didn't clear up my confusion. Why weren't the wise virgins willing to share their oil with the foolish ones, or at least invite them to walk in the light of their lamps? Why wouldn't the bridegroom let them in? How could he be so hard-hearted? Didn't his actions, and those of the wise virgins, contradict everything you'd said about compassion and mercy? Was the one mistake of the foolish virgins so unforgiveable?*
>
> *Slowly I started to understand that being prepared to welcome who one awaits is not about having*

enough; it is about loving enough. Only when I began to understand that the "oil" you spoke of was "love," did I begin to understand what you meant. It is only love that cannot be given for someone else to use; only love that cannot be borrowed from others to light our way.

The foolish virgins did not love enough to wait longer than they'd anticipated. They were not prepared for falling off their carefully drawn map about what and when things should happen. They did not think about needing more love than what they already believed was necessary.

I too so often believe I already love enough, only to fall off my maps and find myself unprepared when things do not happen as I expect or desire. Yet, no one else can fill me with love's energy. Only love (i.e., "oil") uniquely suited to my own heart can light my way to miracles.

I'm still not sure I fully understand. I still have so much more to learn about this lesson.

Crying Out Day and Night

"...every prayer, whatever we ask for and whatever words we may use—or even when we use no words is a call for mercy, [Infinite Light and Love's] gift of unconditional love." (I. Zaleski)

As time went on it gradually became easier to discern the outline of something bigger behind my own small pieces of heaven on earth. Even so, more often than not, my glimpses of the whole were obscured by my attention to what I judged remained incomplete. I discovered I was in good company as I read about the desperate people described in the New Testament, who in seeking the miracle they desired, "barged into private dinners, screamed at Jesus until they had his attention, or destroyed the roof of someone's house to get to him." [59] I was familiar with the stories of these people, of course, but I had always identified more with their urgency and their desperation (*what* drove them to do what they did) than with their faith (*why* they did what they did).

Now I noticed something I'd not noticed before. Those desperate people never sacrificed their perception of the fullness of the miracle they sought. They neither shut down nor turned away in the face of obstacles and even outright denials. Instead, they resolutely witnessed to the reality of their miracle, seeming to see it luminously shining though enfolded in shadow and apparently impossible. They did not act solely out of desperation as I'd first thought. They acted out of an utter and unshakeable belief in the realization of the miracle they sought. Even though as yet unfulfilled, they held their focus firmly and without question on its full emergence.

As I read their stories, I sought to shift from rooting my own perceptions in desperation to anchoring them in an unquestioned sense of the miracle already present, waiting only to be fully revealed in its own time. Gradually, I came to understand that prayer rooted in the quality of relationship between the energy of heaven on earth and our own conscious awareness of that relationship brings the ability to behold the edges of unimagined miracles and draw them out into substance and time.

Loudly

There is a story about Brer Rabbit in the briar patch that I first heard from my father. It is a story that tells of Brer Rabbit saying he does not want what he actually wants for fear that it will be taken from him. The message I heard was clear (if maybe not the one my father intended): pretend you do not want what you really want. I learned this lesson more deeply than my father ever intended or perhaps even knew. As I continued to ponder the reality of Infinite Light and Love incarnate in my life, I began to question whether I, like the desperate people in scripture, shouldn't instead be crying out my dreams loudly, persistently and even boldly.

These ancient people were united in their refusal to be silenced no matter what those around them said or tried to do. They were certain of the validity of their longing and resolute in their conviction that they must be heard. I, on the other hand, found it difficult to remain certain of the validity of my longing in the face of what I could not yet see or what others said. This was in fact what had silenced my soul's song as a child. Even now I found it challenging to keep in sight the wholeness that fed the depths of my heart's desire. It was easier and felt safer for me to keep quiet and retreat, limiting myself to only more of what I could already see.

I remembered one scripture story in particular. It told of a Canaanite woman who asked Jesus loudly for mercy for her daughter even though she repeatedly got no response. Jesus' disciples grew tired of her plea and went to him to ask him to send her away. And Jesus himself said that he was sent only to the lost sheep of Israel. The women persisted, however, and continued to plead loudly for mercy. Jesus then tells her that it is not good to give children's bread to dogs. Undeterred, the woman responds that even dogs feed on crumbs from their masters' tables. On hearing that, Jesus commends her faith and tells her that he shall do as she asks, and her daughter is healed "at once." It was not difficult to imagine myself as an apostle at that scene. I too have been often accused of being too insistent and loud.

<u>Scripture Meditation: The Canaanite Woman</u> *(Matthew 15: 22-28)*

> *I remember this event so well. There we were, walking with you, only to have her loud voice pierce our ears repeatedly. I agreed with your first response, she had no right to ask anything of you. Your second response*

> *only seemed to cement the outcome. Now that I think back, though, I seem to remember a small twinkle in your eyes as you uttered those words, "I was sent only to the lost sheep of Israel." She must have noticed it too for she came right back with her request. And now, everyone around us was waiting to see what you would do. Her next words humbled us all. She asked for crumbs, clearly acknowledging the power of even a small gesture from you. It was that humility, which stood out in contrast to her loud insistence, to which I think you responded with your next statement. "O woman, your faith is great; it shall be done for you as you wish." Her faith was indeed great. I stopped to remember how much even your smallest gestures had come to mean to me. I had not told you that. I had not cried out my love for you. I had been afraid. I am learning.*

Persistently

I didn't know why my miracle seemed to remain incomplete for so long. I started to think that the phrase "seventy times seventy" needed to be applied not just to forgiveness but to prayer as well. I began to suspect that perhaps, like a dancer practicing only every other day, my own inconsistency had something to do with it.

I started to wonder if perhaps the gift of the delay was time to persist, to remain consistent in my belief that I might grow strong enough to receive my miracle in all its radiance without trying to possess or limit it. I don't know if I'll ever know for certain but I do know that radiance has only grown as I've persisted.

I remembered another scripture story about waiting without ceasing to plead one's case. It is a story that highlights another persistent woman, a widow this time. This widow lived in a city where there was a judge who apparently neither respected man nor feared God. Unfortunately, it was from this very judge that the widow needed relief, so she kept repeatedly coming to him asking for legal protection from an opponent. This has always been one of my favorite stories. I revisited it as I thought about the scenario.

Scripture Meditation: The Widow and the Judge *(Luke 18: 1-5)*

> *I was in a similar situation once, repeatedly asking for something I desired. It only got me into trouble though, and so I became afraid. Looking back now, I can see that while I asked persistently, I did not pray persistently. I wonder now if perhaps the widow prayed rather than pleaded. She seemed to have no doubt the judge could and would grant her request. And I know that asking with conviction is entirely different from asking without conviction.*
>
> *Did the judge start to find himself hearing and repeating the widow's words as he went about his work, haunted by the deep conviction in her voice or perhaps with what he could hear as only shrillness? Or perhaps it was just the sheer number of times he'd heard those words that was too much? When she was not there, did he find himself expecting to see her any minute? I don't know. I only know that at first he didn't pay attention to her. Then, after a while, after he seemed to realize that the widow would keep bothering him until she would eventually wear him out, he decided that he would, for that reason—not out of respect for man or fear of God—give her the legal protection she sought.*
>
> *What I am starting to understand now is that I need to do more than simply repeat my prayers, I must pray persistently and with heart through my fear.*

Boldly

After a while, praying loudly and persistently were not so hard for me to do. But there remained one additional quality—boldness. So often I found myself pleading (or was it whining?) loudly and persistently. No one can plead or whine boldly, however. There is always a thread of unbelief about whining and pleading that undermines the very Light and Love it seeks. Boldness requires confident belief.

It took me a while to get in touch with the depths of unbelief in myself. I believed I'd already uprooted it all, yet here it was, doggedly clouding my realization of Infinite Light and Love. I wanted to believe, I really did. I just couldn't seem to sustain confidence in my own believing.

Now, as I found the courage to seek Infinite Light and Love boldly, layer after layer of unbelief emerged. Perhaps that's what I feared about seeking Infinite Light and Love boldly—that I'd first have to face things I didn't want to face. My whole life seemed to dismantle once again when all I wanted was for it to come together. Like layers of an onion, each layer of unbelief seemed to be the last. Then another would appear, constricting my heart and damping my soul's song. I tried to capture the sense of my struggle in two poems. I wrote the first one as I pondered the non-sense of being bold in the absence of affirming evidence.

It Makes No Sense, They Say

Everyone said there was no heaven on earth
Everyone said it was only an illusion
    and I,
    only a fool to think that I could follow my dream of returning there

They said I was only a dreamer
That Love Incarnate walked this earth no more

They made sense, I thought,
And I could find no words to prove them wrong
no matter how hard I argued

Still, my heart struggled to keep believing
Dying just a bit every time my believing faltered
"It doesn't make sense"
"It will only lead you astray"

Still, my heart persistently whispered a sensed reality that defied all sense
Caught between the two
Stretched on the cross
I cried out its voice like a prayer

I turned to St. John of the Cross, a Christian mystic I'd long loved, as I wrote the second poem paraphrasing what I was only now starting to understand:

Dark Night, Full of Light[60]

On a dark night
My doubts and fears silenced and still
I left unnoticed
My heart on fire
Impatient and restless to find
Love's Light unending

Dark night
When hope is chosen
without reason
without evidence
Spurred by heart's desire

Hidden, disguised
I stepped out into night's embrace

without light
without guide
Led by heart's illumination

Guided certainly
To where I knew yet could not know
To where what is sought
what calls heart to heart
Waits patiently to be met
To transform and unite

Dark night, full of light
When love goes out in hope
And faith is forged
to flame in darkness
and make believing more than make-believe

Enfold me in your grace

I remembered a scripture story about a host who rushed out boldly in the middle of the night to ask a neighbor for a favor. A friend has just arrived, delayed way past the expected time he'd said he'd come. The host finds that he has no food to set before his friend, who is tired and hungry. He goes out to his neighbor to ask him for three loaves. The neighbor has already gone to bed, however, and doesn't even get up. He merely calls out, "Don't bother me. It's late, we're all already in bed and I cannot get up to give you anything." Fortunately, like the son in another scripture story who first said no to his father and then changed his mind, the neighbor also changes his mind and says yes though not, the story notes, out of friendship but because of his friend's boldness. I imagined myself in a similar scenario.

<u>Scripture Meditation: Asking a Friend for Bread</u> *(Luke11: 5-8)*

Unlike the friend in the story, I feared going to you at midnight to knock on your door. I guess I didn't yet fully trust your friendship, so unlike any I'd ever known before. What if you didn't answer? Or, worse yet, woke up only to shut the door in my face? Pray persistently and insistently you said. I heard that message. But pray boldly—rush out in the middle of the night? Wasn't that carrying trusting a bit too far?

I chewed on Jesus' words and a deeper meaning emerged. In them I started to hear an invitation to release, not my hope or desire, but the frustration and desperation that kept me praying timidly, tied to only what was already present and blind to heaven's greater Light and Love. Ironically, it is the fullness of my hope and desire I surrender when I pray without boldness—in the very effort to prevent that surrender. I had it all turned around.

Just recently I came across a story that added another dimension to my understanding of praying boldly: the story of Honi, the Jewish circle maker.[61] *It is said that during a severe drought that threated both the lives and livelihood of the villagers in the area, Honi went outside and drew a circle. He stepped into the circle, telling God that he would stay there, praying for rain, until God granted his prayer. As if that wasn't enough, when it started to rain lightly, he boldly told God he needed a heavier rain—and, then, when it started to storm, he told God that wasn't quite right either, that he wanted only a steady downpour that would nourish without destroying. Wow! Only a deep intimacy with God could keep such bold behavior from becoming offensive or arrogant. And that's when*

I got it. Praying boldly first requires the deep intimacy cultivated by persistent loving.

With Trembling Heart

"Love like there's no tomorrow, and if tomorrow comes, love again."
(M. Lucado)

There is a story told about a disciple traveling with his Master.[62] When the disciple voiced his thirst, his Master told him to drink from the sea. Instead, the disciple poured water from the sea into a flask. Seeing this his Master asked him why he did that. The disciple answered that he wanted to make sure he'd have water to drink not just now but also when he got thirsty later. In reply, the Master gently told him to remember that God was not only here, in the sea, God was also everywhere.

Like that disciple I so often found myself clinging to the Infinite Light and Love I experienced, bottling them so that I "won't be thirsty later on." I struggled to remember that it is not containing and preserving that assures no thirst. Rather, it is trusting Infinite Love and Light enough to ask "What is there of Infinite Love and Light for me in what is here now?"

Don't Look Back

The challenge to let go was not new. I realized now, though, that while I knew <u>how</u> to let go, I did not yet KNOW letting go. I recalled once reading that love is the absence of defenses. I started to understand what I had only intermittently intuited before: that what was critical was not the act of letting go (the what) so much as the quality of letting go (the how). It was the intimate KNOWING of the Infinite Light and Love that fed that act that was essential, even when letting go was done with a trembling heart. Letting go invited me not into forced release or blind submission but into the intimate embrace of *wholeness*—into reality freed from the constraints of illusion. It opened me to become one with Infinite Light and Love within me and all around me.

I realized I'd focused on doing letting go rather than KNOWING letting go. With this realization, I began to perceive letting go not as a forced loss but as a deep opening of self to intimacy. I then KNEW the substance of letting go as *reconciliation* rather than submission. It was not about giving up, it was about diving in.

I started to understand that true letting go comes from a place of union rather than one of division. Letting go came almost without effort when I attended to love and light as one whole with the assurance that nothing but that love and light was necessary because everything was already held within it.

I started to learn to let go of what I'd clung to, not out of blind commitment but out of open-heartedness, not as a means to an end but as an affirmation of that end: YES! to continuing and deepening my initial YES! ...to the fullness of heaven on earth, which so unexpectedly returned into my life; ...to the Love and Light that holds me within it; ...to embracing the unique shape of both friendship and Spirit in presence and absence; ...to the growing body of my miracle as it emerged into its own fullness through growing acts of letting go.

I remembered a scripture story that had always haunted me. It is about two men who, on hearing Jesus' call to follow him, ask for permission to first complete some duty or task. The first asks for permission to go bury his father, which seemed only natural to me. The second asks for permission to go say good-bye to his parents since he is leaving, perhaps forever. Jesus says to both that no one who looks back after putting his hand to the plow is fit for God's kingdom. I remembered that story and began to reflect on hearing its words as if spoken directly to me.

Scripture Meditation: Don't Stop to Bury the Dead *(Luke 9: 59-62)*

Your words made no sense, not when I first heard them. It was only as your invitation kept nudging my heart that I started to understand and KNOW the meaning of following you in an entirely different way. To follow: to embrace wholly, without looking back to furrows already plowed, old patterns of action and reaction that split reality; to live out the fullness of God's face incarnate on earth, faithfully rendering it into form and space though still in shadow.

I caught a glimpse of the fact that such following required something more than simply walking beside you, still carrying my old identity and letting it define me. One of your apostles later called it walking in Christ rather than walking with Christ. Perhaps that was it, a bit like being in love. We talked about that once. The person who loves gives and receives love as a distinct quality—and that is good. The person in love is immersed in its current, indistinguishable from it, living it fully—and that is a miracle!

I am only beginning to learn how to not look back to already plowed ground. I am only beginning to learn how to live on earth without losing heaven and how to live in heaven without losing earth—at least until I die (and perhaps not even then). To believe in God enough to follow without looking back takes making believing more than make believe.[63]

Without Money or a Walking Stick

I remember when I was first recalled into a love I had stopped believing could really be. Heaven come to earth! How could I not follow? I didn't look back then, not at first, not until I started to stumble across new ground with no familiar paths, not until your love opened long locked doors.

The subtle persistence of heaven and earth as still somehow irreconcilable, which had stopped me then, surfaced again. I felt unprepared, without sufficient resources. My responses shifted between two alternatives: lifting earth, where I could find the resources I thought I needed, "up" into heaven or bringing heaven, unpredictable and uncontrollable Infinite Light and Love, "down" to earth. Only recently have I come to know that it is never about choosing between lifting earth (human light and love) up or bringing heaven (Infinite Light and Love) down. It is instead about trusting enough to release the split ground that holds and nourishes the root of their separation.

I meditated on a second scripture story that talked about following. It was one that, like the one I'd read earlier, also set a bar I didn't believe I could meet. This story was about when Jesus sent his disciples out on their first solitary mission. He instructed them to carry neither money, nor bag, nor shoes; to not even greet anyone along the way and to wish peace only after entering into a home. All means of support or relief were to be unavailable to them until they entered into a home. Once again, it seemed to say that following required a level of surrender beyond any I believed I could reach. I imagined myself hearing Jesus' words once again.

Scripture Meditation: Sending the Seventy *(Luke 10: 3-6)*

> *There it was: the invitation to actively unite my vision with yours, the challenge to live your way without relying on resources of my own. My first response was "Really? You've got to be kidding!" I already felt so vulnerable, loving you in a world that did not understand. Now you wanted me to step out without the objects of my security.*

I was afraid to go and yet I knew I couldn't stay. It had been the fullness of my love for you and yours for me that had led me here. Now, only the fullness of faith could fulfill the promise of that love. You didn't tell us to be without fear this time, perhaps because you wanted us to plumb the depths of fear that kept us from heaven on earth. I learned about my fear as I traversed its terrain, setting out as you'd asked.

And, miracle of miracles, I returned full of joy. I remembered the words of a fellow traveler that even demons were subject to us in your name. I think I understand exactly what he meant. I too had faced demons of fear, anxiety, impatience, frustration and doubt, and watched them disappear, dissolved in Infinite Light and Love.

I've come full circle, hearing Your call asking me to follow you into the fullness of what I only glimpsed before, in our first encounter. I've heard it said that such following is less about staying within the lines and more about saying Yes to the joy that comes from the following.

When a friend follows a friend for the sheer joy of the companionship, everything and anything necessary to remain immersed in that joy is then freely offered as gift. In the midst of a journey taken without money or provisions, fear pales beside the need to follow a love so deep and so true that the limits of possibility are transcended: people walk on water, the blind see, the lame walk and the dead return to life.

Perhaps that's closer to the fullness of faith you desire so deeply for me. I'm still learning. I only know that my soul sings when I hear your voice calling to me.

No Longer Alone

With each step of my journey, just when I thought I'd reached my limits my love deepened. "Yes" stretched my hope and grew my faith. Falling in love and following that love into the Infinite Light and Love it mirrored awakened a deeper *me* nestled and nurtured within my soul, part and parcel of that same Light and Love yet somehow still me. Perhaps, this me is the *me* that resides in and is defined by what Thomas Merton calls "le point vierge," a sacred space deep within each of us, untouched by ego or human distortion.[64] It is, I believe, a space given to each of us to hold and carry both Infinite Light and Love and our truest self forever innocent and inviolate.

I read the words of one apostle about Christ living in him: *"The life you see me living is not 'mine"*(Galatians 2:19-20). It is a life lived in Christ, my Beloved, who loves me and gives himself for and to me. I imagined talking with Jesus about that.

<u>Scripture Meditation: Christ Lives in Me</u> *(Galatians 2:20)*

> *Sometimes I've thought your words were all about changing my behavior. Other times I'd thought that they meant giving up my very soul and being left with no room for my dearest and deepest self. Either way, up until now I've believed that they were meant only for super-spiritual people and required giving up much more than I could ever give up. I've thought I had to become someone other than myself, much holier and with fewer faults, leaving behind my preferences and human be-ing. I believed that reality lay somewhere in the distant future, once I became a saint (and stopped caring so much about being human), if I ever became a saint. It was sort of like believing I could traverse the world in one night once I became Santa Claus!*

I am now beginning to catch glimpses of what you were really saying. I see their meaning more clearly, though I still can't really say them about myself. I am hearing the sounds of a new meaning, one that does not ask me to split me—and all I hold dear—from you in order to embrace and be embraced by your love.

Just as I finished writing the sentence above, I opened my email to find these words: "To see the world while hearing Christ's heartbeat."[65] *Perhaps these words capture a bit of the true meaning of your words. They certainly capture a bit of what I now understand. To hear someone's heartbeat, as John did at that last supper, when he leaned upon your breast is to be so intimately in communion that we "co-live" and are never just ourselves, by ourselves, ever again.*

Three Steps Forward, Two Steps Back:

MOVING TO THE MUSIC

"Life itself—and scripture too—is always three steps forward and two steps backward." **(R. Rohr)** *"It's a frustrating way to make progress but it's a wonderful way to dance."* **(J. Cainer)**

Boldly praying a consistent and insistent "Yes" through unmapped territory reconnected me with my own deepest and truest self, with the love offered me, and with the fullness of Infinite Light and Love within which both were held. I literally fell in love all over again. Less dependent on needing to have a specific map, I allowed myself to simply enjoy—and en-joy (i.e., in-carnate joy)—the friendship to which my friend remained committed even after he verbalized his decision not to marry.

My soul's song became stronger in response to my repeated "Yes." My journey became dance, its joys clearer and brighter. I thought I'd arrived. I assumed that my "greatest trials [were] over, and with [but] a bit of gentle shepherding, everything [would] somehow proceed naturally in a positive direction."[66]

But life—and deep friendship—surprised me once more. As the truth of Infinite Light and Love present and active on earth became ever more evident, sustaining it unexpectedly became more difficult and out of reach. Unwavering belief seemed within my grasp only to evaporate like morning's dew in the heat of a burning sun. Old fears I'd thought laid to rest long before rose again: heaven on earth was neither of my making nor within my control, how could it be trusted? I had little experience with benign realities outside my making and control to present as evidence against those fears. Like a swimmer who has come to terms with water but still cannot trust its buoyancy enough to just let go, I'd learned to float yet remained on full alert, ready to return to determined swimming at a moment's notice.

I realized that at a deep level I had yet to trust that Infinite Light and Love offers incredible and unearned love, beauty, awe and wonder amid and within the inspirations and confusions of our soul. I began to believe that heaven could not *be* without earth. To separate heaven (i.e., love, beauty, awe, wonder) from earth's trials is "to lose the personal intimacy" of God's infinite self playing through the chords of my being. To separate earth's trials from heaven is "to lose the cosmic vastness" of Infinite Light and Love within which their sting can be softened. Together, earth's flawed and limited notes echo "within the glory and birth pangs of the universe," and vice versa. [67]

Though I'd learned to see both sides of these dualities previously on my journey, I became aware of just how strongly I continued to hold on to distinct preferences that inevitably led me to make a choice of half over whole. I'd rejoiced then in the communion of heaven and earth. Yet, even so, the underlying dichotomies remained, subtly shadowing that communion: here vs. there, now vs. then (or soon), mappable vs. unmappable, arrived vs. not there yet. Gradually, as I stopped to pay attention to what always felt like three steps forward and two steps backwards, I began to understand that while the third step forward kept me going, it was the two steps back that kept me whole.

Three challenges came to the fore as I reflected on that, inviting me to transcend my contradictions, go beyond boundaries set by my mind, and transform my back and forth rhythm into dance.

Contradictions Transcended

"The resolution doesn't lie in collapsing the tension of opposites by canceling one of them out. Something has to go deeper, something that can hold them both."
(C. Bourgeault)

"It is a disciplined practice of placing oneself in between two worlds, or at the midpoint between two extremes that seem irreconcilable, and faithfully waiting until the intersecting of their shared essence occurs."
(J. P. Newell)

It has been said that the only legitimate understanding of faith is one that leaves us off balance and unsure of ourselves.[68] It certainly felt that way to me, something that said "let go" just when I believed holding on was the one thing that allowed me to survive, and then reversed itself to insist that I hold on when letting go seemed the only possible response. Like Nachson facing the Red Sea,[69] I felt called to jump into a sea I did not believe I could swim.

I remembered a story about a man who was in a terrible hurry as he traveled through Africa.[70] This man, the story says, pushed his African helpers to keep moving day after day, telling them they could not afford to stop. They traveled in this way for many days until finally the helpers simply stopped and dropped to the ground. No matter what the man told them, they refused to get up. When the man questioned them, they replied that they had moved too quickly and now needed to wait to give their spirits a chance to catch up.

Up until now, when what I considered forward progress stopped, I'd felt ejected from paradise, unable to keep heaven and earth connected or even perceive the possibility of connection. Thrown off by the difference between what was present before me and what I envisioned, I'd race ahead, afraid to remain with dissonance, fearing it belied the truth I'd glimpsed. Now I began to wonder if in my fear that the aspects of my journey in which I'd come to delight would be canceled out by those within which I could find no delight, I too was leaving pieces of my spirit behind on the roadside, some forgotten, others injured and in pain, some simply not valued as necessary to where I wanted to be. Perhaps my "two steps back" were an invitation to stop and wait for my spirit to catch up.

Presence and Absence

The apparent contradiction between presence and absence was one that repeatedly pulled me two steps back. The harmony between the two emerged haltingly as I reflected on my clinging to one and resisting the other. At first, I focused solely on presence. I loved the experience of presence and wanted to remain within it always. My friend's presence affirmed my soul's song and called me into my journey, gradually becoming sacrament for a greater Presence.

When we could not be together and I could not sense that presence, however, absence became all too real, casting me into fear and anxiety. I perceived absence only as the negation of presence, both human and divine. If I couldn't experience presence it must be gone. To cling to it in the midst of experienced absence was too painful, a reminder of what was not. Gradually, though, I found that presence always returned.[71]

Gradually, I learned to endure absence and await the return of presence. As I did, the continued tension between presence and absence somehow evolved into more than I could have anticipated. Bit by bit, the parts of me that could not bear to even think of presence in the middle of absence started to heal. I began to find the deeper truth of presence as I quite literally re-membered it, not as something lost but as something that somehow remained true even when I could not sense it.

At the same time I discovered a different kind of understanding and perceiving that showed me absence not as the mere emptiness of vanished presence but as pregnant space holding presence yet to be born. When I stayed present to that space I discovered that nothing was ever actually lost. When I could not do that, absence showed me the places in me yet unhealed. It was then that I realized the inextricable complementarity between presence and absence. Without presence absence becomes only emptiness, devoid of life and love, without God, without heaven. Without absence, presence loses its capacity for intimacy and becomes only what we can possess and control.

I'd yearned for the reality of unconditional love yet had never fully embraced it, pulled back by my fear of losing it. I'd believed there was less pain to losing when something (or someone) is never fully embraced, not realizing that in keeping myself from ever really experiencing that embrace I'd merely experienced the losing all along. Now, I began to find enduring presence, both touchable and beyond touch. In the seeming absence of all external evidence, the fullness of love—both visible and invisible—emerged.

I think perhaps it might have the same for the apostles. They too experienced presence, struggled with absence, and discovered a presence within that absence deeper than any they'd ever anticipated or known. I remembered Jesus' tri-fold challenge to Peter: "Do you love me, Simon, son of John? Do you love me? Do you love me?" It was not a horizontal challenge; i.e., the same question asked repeatedly. It was a vertical challenge: each question digging just a little deeper. I replayed the scene in my imagination as if I was Peter.

Scripture Meditation: Peter, Do You Love Me *(John 21:15, 16; 17)*

> *You said "I am with you always." Yet, how could I believe when you were already saying you would leave, and I was already starting to sense your absence? Was it all illusion after all? So many said so. A fool, they called me. "Be real," they said. They all agreed. Yet here you were, recalling me to the love between us. Did I love you? Of course I loved you. Did I love you deeply and truly enough to believe unconditionally, without fear? I thought I did. Did I believe deeply enough to surrender my fear? I wanted to.*
>
> *Your friendship meant everything to me. Imperfectly as I understood or could respond, it was still all I'd ever dreamed of. I remembered God's words to Adam and Eve: "Where are you?" Troubled and fearful, they could not see the reality of the garden you had so tenderly created for them even as they stood within it. They clung to their idea of God, blind to God's idea of and for them! Perhaps I was not so different from them.*
>
> *I remembered that, through it all, God remained. And now you asked me if I would remain, if I would*

allow your love to enfold me and unfold within me. You knew that I loved you deeply and fully. It was me who had forgotten.

Yes, three times yes. I love you. I love you. I love you. I will follow my soul's song into the mystery of your presence-less presence. I will move to its rhythm as it sings to me of your love. I will walk this walk because I can't not walk it. Slowly, I entered further into a mystery, and that changed everything. Freed from the constraints of my five senses by the gift of absence, I started forward again. In and through that reality I discovered the fullness of love.

Knowing and Unknowing

Underlying my polarization of presence and absence was a subtle, and sometimes not so subtle, resistance to moving beyond the certainty of foreknowledge and guarantees. As my experience of absence transformed, though, so did my knowing. As absence invited me beyond presence, unknowing invited me beyond a simple cognitive understanding into the depths of mystery. In the midst of uncertainty, if I allowed myself to stop and wait, I found hope emerging to invite me to meet Infinite Light and Love in mystery, wonder, and bewilderment beyond what even my wildest dreams could contain.

Amazingly, not knowing (i.e., unknowing) became the doorway into deep intimacy, a deeper knowing that lay just beyond the strictures of my certainty. I remembered words I'd once read "...a journey that begins ineffably can only be fulfilled ineffably, which is to say, fulfilled unforeseeably in ways that overflow anything we might think or imagine our fulfillment to be."[72]

In embracing unknowing I found the parts of myself that my homemade self, itself judged and cast out, had judged and cast out in its effort to once again experience the love it so yearned for. Paradoxically, these parts, like Adam and Eve, felt too naked to allow the embrace of the very love they so deeply desired. I recognized now that what repeatedly got in the way was not my limitations or my failures, but my unwillingness to allow Infinite Light and Love to come into contact with those limitations and failures.[73]

I turned to scripture to an account of the apostles being asked who they believed Jesus was. Perhaps they were asked like I was now being asked to attend to mystery not with the knowing of their minds but with the knowing intuited by their hearts. How would have I answered then? How would I answer now if Jesus asked me who I believed he was?

<u>Scripture Meditation: Who Do You Say I Am?</u> *(Luke 9:20)*

> *I was so often frustrated when You talked about not knowing: not knowing when a thief would come; not knowing when the bridegroom would come; not knowing how seeds sprout and grow. I wanted to know. It took me a long time to begin to understand that the knowing I believed I needed was not the knowing you desired for me.*
>
> *Judas could not understand. To him it was just about expensive oil "wasted." The Pharisees could not understand. To them it was all about the law. Yet the woman anointing your feet in the middle of a meal, against all the rules of right and wrong, knew. She knew without question, as did the farmer who sowed a mustard seed against all law and reason. The rich young man could not understand. Hadn't he already followed all the rules? But the blind man, moving toward you without eyesight, knew.*
>
> *Now you asked me: Who did I believe you to be? Many voices within and without clamored for*

my attention as I heard your question, like children waving their hands to be recognized by the teacher. The voice of my mind believed it knew the answer. It spoke up with all reason, asking for understanding and proof. It was quickly joined by other voices speaking their judgments and conclusions. The voice of my own doubts joined in, equally firm in its knowing, pointing out the differences between what I wanted you to do and what you did. How could you be whom I believed you to be if you did not do what I wished for so deeply?

Amid the clamor of those voices, the quiet voice of my heart, resonating to your love, whispered of a different kind of knowing that needed neither understanding nor proof, nor desired behaviors. My fingers, once so tightly curled around only what I could understand, slowly uncurled, one by one, like a bud opening to the sun's light.

Believing in me, you did not wait for me to believe. Receiving and holding dear every experience and every touch you did not hold on. Yet neither did you let go as you let all that was divine define you and dance through you (and me): your gift to God and God's to you—as well as to me. Who did I believe you to be? I can neither understand nor imagine. I can only KNOW. You are my Beloved.

Holding On and Letting Go

As my clinging to presence against absence and knowing against unknowing loosened, the deeper roots of my fear were revealed: a holding on to life that paradoxically constrained my living. I'd lived for so long believing I feared dying. I wondered now if perhaps I'd not instead been dying fearing living. At some level, I'd always

KNOWN that I was constraining the very life of my life, beset by a fear that belied my believing and kept image apart from reality. I believed, but only from a distance, removed from my own deepest truth, real yet not real enough to inhabit fully.[74]

For me the contradiction between holding on and letting go was a given. One day, though, I realized it was that very contradiction that kept Infinite Love and Light suspended just out of reach, almost literally in mid-air. I started to see the contradiction between holding on to my life and letting go of my life for the illusion that it was. Only someone who is thinking in terms of possession focuses on what to hold on to and what to release. I started to ask myself if I really wanted to live Infinite Light and Love or if I only wanted to possess them. I stayed at this point in my journey for a long time, praying that, like two photographs merged into one, my *image* of Infinite Light and Love might be reconciled with the *reality* of Infinite Light and Love in my life.

Suddenly I realized that was exactly what was happening each time I experienced the contradiction between holding on (i.e., living) and letting go (i.e., dying). It was an experience that put me in touch with the depths of my yearning while at the same time placing me squarely in its impossibility—two distinct images in sharp contrast: what I wanted and what I perceived to be. Perhaps the idea was not so much to choose between them but to hold both simultaneously, allowing their reconciliation and integration to evolve on its own. Perhaps I could allow the paradox of living and dying to be just that, a paradox.

It was one thing for me to believe and even to start to experience the split within me beginning to heal. It was another to let desire blossom into substance. I closed my eyes and turned in trust to Infinite Light and Love asking neither to hold on to life nor to let it go. I wasn't certain what would come next; I only knew that I had to allow Infinite Light and Love to be, not in passive submission but in radical celebration of a love and a knowing not quite my own yet given to me.

The communion of presence and absence brought me into the fullness of love; the communion of knowing and unknowing revealed the fullness of hope; the communion of holding on and letting go came more slowly and brought with it the fullness of faith.

I returned to scripture to search for words that echoed this new-to-me conscious and sustained bearing of the love reflected in Beloved's gaze. There they were, familiar words about letting go of one's life to find it. I imagined I was hearing your words spoken directly to me.

Scripture Meditation: For Who Would Save His Life *(Matthew 16:25)*

> *When I first heard your words about losing my life, they struck fear into my heart. I believed you were advocating a loss of all I'd ever held dear. Despite my belief in and love for you, deep uneasiness stirred within me every time I heard those words. For a long time they triggered only inhibited trust and limited faith.*
>
> *Until, one day, my uneasiness abated. I don't fully understand what happened or how it happened. Perhaps I never will. What I do know is that I finally heard your words differently. I heard the distinction between a self lost and a self loosened, from a self severed from self and a self loosened from the grip of all that has held and defined it so tightly, ironically a self already severed, apart and alone.*
>
> *Surrendering—loosening—what had held me in bondage for so long, however frightening, was a "losing" I'd gladly embrace. Understood in this way, it was the natural outcome of first yielding into what freed me, like a dancer yielding to the music that sets her heart to singing. It was in fact this very yielding*

that first called me, though I had not known it then as I do now. It was not about my will, enclosed by what I know and want and imagine; rather it was about yours—the music of Infinite Light and Love, which resonates in my heart, yours yet mine, given to me and in me.

Metanoia

*"and the decisive breakthrough is not so much in what [we] see as in **how** [we] see"* (C. Bourgeault)

The common understanding of "metanoia" is "beyond mind." I'd read this many times; "change your mind and believe such good news."[75] Yet, it took time and struggle to me to realize that metanoia was not simply about changing *what* I thought. It was more about changing *how* I thought. It involved a shift from seeing the world through the lens of my mind (mind-sight) to seeing it through the eyes of my heart (heart-sight). The mind can only know *about* what it perceives. It cannot truly KNOW what it perceives (i.e., become intimate with it).

I had long used my mind's perception (i.e., mind-sight) to orient to my world. The challenge now was to learn to use heart's perception, to go beyond my mind and see what I could not through mental understanding. In a way, perhaps, that was exactly what I'd been searching for in my earlier "wrestling with God."[76]

Blindsight

As I was reflecting on metanoia I serendipitously found references to the phenomenon of *blindsight*, a type of seeing that bypasses the physical means of the eye while still allowing access to a perception of what is physically around us. A person with blindsight, for example, can reach for things and walk without running into obstacles even though physically blind. While not comprehensible to the mind this type of seeing is nevertheless inclusive of it, providing it with verifiable data it can accept (e.g., one doesn't run into things). One of the clearest descriptions of blindsight comes from Jacques Lussyran's book, *And There Was Light*. Blinded in childhood, Lusseyran recounts how he discovered the ability to see in a totally unexpected way.

The phenomenon of blindsight provided me with a timely metaphor for seeing with my heart what I could not see with my mind. I started to trust my believing—what my heart discerned—not as a mental assertion to a known "visible" fact but as a simple soul[77] who accepts truth without need for analysis, proof, or decision. In simply loving and loving simply the Infinite Light and Love of which my soul sang broke open into visible outcome and form.

As I turned to scripture, I wondered if perhaps it was the same for the apostles. As they faced the reality of Jesus' resurrection, they too found themselves needing to go beyond what their minds could perceive or conceive. "He is risen," they were told, "His tomb is empty." Yet, could it be true? How could they believe what they knew (with their minds) was impossible even as their hearts were stirred and filled with an inexpressible joy. Perhaps they too "turned around" from mind to heart. I imagined myself as someone who had been there with them, hearing of Jesus' resurrection.

<u>Scripture Meditation: Even Though You Do Not See Him Now</u>
(Mark 16:6; 1 Peter 1:8)

> *Mary Magdalene had rushed to your burial site to see you once more. She had seen you there, she said. You appeared to your apostles. Even Thomas, who did not believe easily, surrendered his doubt as he came face to face with you. All found tangible proof of*

> *your continued presence, though not in any way they'd anticipated.*
>
> *Yet, I couldn't seem to find such proof. Neither my sight nor my touch revealed your continued reality to me. My belief in your life remained indefensible and outside the realm of direct experience. Still, now and then there were those times when, unexpected and unexplainable, it seemed as if I could see and touch you. But was that real? Or was it simply my imagination providing me with what I so deeply yearned for? My heart believed. My mind questioned. What if I let myself believe and it turned out to only be illusion? What if I continued to doubt and missed your presence entirely? I felt I had to choose one or the other, yet that too seemed impossible.*
>
> *I don't know exactly how or when it happened, when you turned my world around and my mind and heart aligned. I only remember that my heart opened (like Mary's) and my mind stopped fighting (like Thomas'). It was then that I started to actually see and touch your living presence. I had had sight yet had been blind.*

Befriending

The mind can know *about* what it perceives. It cannot, however, befriend what it perceives. Only the heart can befriend. Befriending is a process beautifully portrayed in *The Little Prince*, St. Exupery's story of believing. When the little prince meets a fox and asks to befriend him, the fox replies that it is first necessary to tame him by coming consistently to be with him. Though the emphasis seems to be on the fox being tamed, the story carries strong hints that the little prince is also being tamed. In a parallel fashion, my heart needed to be tamed so that it might feel safe enough to come out of hiding and share its deep KNOWING without fear. Equally, my mind needed to learn to befriend my heart so that it might more easily and fully accept its KNOWING.

The heaven (Infinite Light and Love) my heart intuited could not be found at the expense of the finite human reality my mind perceived. Yet, neither could that reality (i.e., earth) be fully lived without heaven. Like a two-part harmony, one part without the other leaves half the song unsung. Only with mind and heart together can Infinite Light and Love shine undiminished within finite human reality. Only with mind and heart together can we open to "the kind of delight and joy that would make our obsession[s]…look like futzing over an airline bag of peanuts when outside our window is Mount Rainer in all her winter glory, waiting for the passenger to look and gasp in amazement."[78]

One spiritual writer gives directions that I find applicable to *befriending*: Remember the place that has awakened within you and turn towards it. Lift it up to the Infinite Light and Love that awakened it and *simply abide there.*[79] I turned toward the place awakened within me time and time again, no matter external circumstances, lifting up all within me that resonated with it.

In this integration of all things into one and in One the broken fragments of my self came together to join in one song, like the colors of a rainbow dancing into one brilliant light. It is the soul song I now KNOW as I once KNEW, without question and, paradoxically, without understanding. I re-membered and once again heard the voice of Divine Beloved, recalling me to the human love that had drawn me in the first place.

Slowly, I learned to stay in touch with the whispers of a fragile faith that remembered and was somehow itself born of a deeper unseen presence perceived through heart-sight. I started to understand why those first apostles, besotted with the love that had come to meet them, repeatedly told others to seek "God's kingdom first." I began to see why they were so insistent that it was necessary to dwell on "things true, noble, reputable, authentic, compelling gracious—the best, note the worst" (Philippians 4:8). I thought of what it might have been like to have lived what they had lived as I imagined myself talking with Divine Beloved.

<u>Scripture Meditation: Seek First God's Kingdom</u> *(Mt. 6:33; Phil. 4:8)*

> *You told us to seek first your kingdom. At first I understood that to mean something like first getting the money for a trip as a means of getting what we needed for life later. And perhaps it did mean that in one way, perhaps it was just the life part I didn't understand.*
>
> *But I didn't get that, not at first. I thought I understood what I was looking for and all I needed to do to head in its direction. I did not anticipate that the kingdom would be neither what nor where I believed it to be—or that your words might have a different meaning. I know you tried to tell us that very thing yet I believed I already knew what the kingdom was if not where.*
>
> *Only as you opened my eyes and I learned to befriend heart's reality did I truly begin to understand. And then I knew that seeking the kingdom was not about learning to get it right. It was about becoming intimate with its extravagant abundance. That's when I remembered the words spoken by one of your apostles about dwelling on what is good and honorable, right and pure. He was saying the same thing.*
>
> *I needed to befriend this kingdom so much more deeply than I'd ever thought. It wasn't about dwell on what I needed to get "there" or on how I might receive more of its riches. It was about dwelling in its very nature, so much more wonderful than I'd let myself*

believe was truly possible, the joy and love it offered so much more immense then I'd imagined or could imagine.

Its nature was so much wilder and freer than any I'd known. It asked not that I embrace its Infinite Light and Love but that I let them embrace me. I was overwhelmed. It was almost too much to take in. It was all I'd ever wanted yet more than I could contain. I started to more deeply understand then why you asked us to seek the kingdom first: not so we might learn to tap its resources and bring them out into our ordinary life but rather that we might learn to yield to and abide in the immensity of its Infinite Light and Love.

Acceptance

As my heart and mind met each other within the embrace of Infinite Light and Love my heart's resistance to becoming vulnerable and my mind's stubborn refusal to let go its need to know and control both loosened. I had feared that losing that resistance and refusal would also somehow silence the joys and wonders of Infinite Light and Love I'd focused on collecting in my pocket, like jewels to bring out in times of doubt.[80] Now, however, I discovered that preserved joys and wonders, like cut flowers, never compare to living realities.

Embracing acceptance slowly became the counterstroke to the challenge of surrender, which had plagued me for so long. The lesson had always been there, in my writing. As a writer I experience a mind-based writer-self that selects words, edits, and generally manages the details of my writing. At the same time I also experience another less verbal more intuitive heart-based self. This self inspires the insights my writer-self puts into words. In order to accept these insights, I need to suspend (i.e., surrender) the writer-self. While neither the writer-self's thinking nor her funds of knowledge are erased, they do have to assume a more proper role in service to the inspiration offered by my intuitive heart-based self. In order to transcend the limits of my writer-self's thoughts and words, I need to become open and accepting of that which gives them life in the first place.

As this insight evolved, I started to focus on accepting gain rather then fearing loss, on bringing the often-disparate visions of my mind, which informed my writer-self, and those of my heart, which offered its wordless intuition, into a single integrated focus. I started allowing a larger and deeper vision as I practiced this integration.

I remembered a scripture story about a grain of wheat (John 12:24). Its message is that unless that grain is buried (i.e., surrendered, "lost"), it can never be transformed into its promise: wheat. That same message resurfaces in another scripture story about a treasure buried in a field. This story tells of a man finding a treasure and then re-burying it. I could not really make sense of it for a long time. Now, I began to understand it as a retelling of that earlier story about the grain of wheat: when form is surrendered, let go in reckless abandon out of sheer joy, then paradoxically, promise can be birthed into form. I started to reflect on that.

Scripture Meditation: The Kingdom Is Like This *(Matthew 13:44)*

> *I remembered the story you'd told, about a man finding a treasure in a field, and finally really heard it, I think. When I'd heard it in the past, I'd focused on the acquisition of the treasure. I'd understood the re-burying of it only as a strategy for ensuring its safekeeping until the man could get what he needed. I'd never thought of it as a surrender necessary to go beyond the single treasure. Now, almost all of a sudden it seemed, my focus shifted from the treasure in the field to the field itself. I started to see the burying of the treasure in light of your words about the grain of*

wheat: the surrender of something into the ground that gives it life. Perhaps it was something like that, like finding a fish and deciding to keep it alive by purchasing the sea rather than taking it out of its proper home and clinging to it as one single fish. As you said: But if you let it go, reckless in your love, you'll have it forever, real and eternal (John 12:25; The Message; emphasis added)

Dancing

"You dance through the world with the Divine Beloved, knowing that whatever you need, one way or another, will always come.
(T. Silver)
"Be wise; cast all your votes for dancing!"
(Hafiz)

With steps forward and steps backward, my journey steadily drew me to dance to the rhythm of my soul's song. I had started my journey believing Infinite Light and Love was a reality beyond me. Then I had come to believe deeply in Infinite Light and Love as a reality reflected both within and around me. Now, I started to understand the need to allow Infinite Light and Love to flow, not just beyond and in me, but also from and through me, as me, an expression of my truest self. The words of Boehme, a 17th century mystic, came back to mind as I moved into this phase of my journey: "I, God, press through your branches into the sap and bear fruit on your boughs."[81]

The centrality of three inner stances became clear as I walked the path before me now: the stance of receiving, forged by and forging deepening love; the stance of yielding, forged by and forging deepening hope; and the stance of KNOWING forged by and forging deepening faith. Each stance was key to transforming endings into beginnings. Sometimes, they just occurred without any effort on my part, as graced moments I could neither command nor control. At other times, they required explicit focus and effort. At all times I sought to remember that each needed to be celebrated unconditionally not as strategies or means to an end but purely for their own value and joy. Dancing could not come without them; yet neither did they control whether it came or not. That was always and ever only gift.

Receiving: Dancing in Deepening Love

The inner stance of receiving emerged as my understanding of mutuality expanded, both forged by and forging deepening love. More than just taking in or getting, I now perceived receiving as rooted in the penetration of a love mutually offered and received, calling forth my deepest and most authentic self while simultaneously leading me beyond it. There are many images for such receiving: a prodigal son's return to his true home and true name (Luke 15: 11-32); a love reaffirmed in response to a thrice-asked question (John 21:16); a woman's outpouring of perfume (Luke 7: 36-50), an unexpected meeting with a beloved friend (my own experience).

Up until now, when "I" had made space to receive Infinite Love and Light, "I" continued to take up that very space, filling rather than being filled. It was a subtle yet striking difference in orientation. Now, love's mutuality insistently and tenderly urged me to stretch my limits beyond that "I" and make space for the gift of Infinite Light and Love even when I did not feel like doing so or could not comprehend how I might do so.

At first, this understanding just seemed to be an echo of what I'd already lived and learned. I sought to discern what was different. I started to wonder just what was, or could be, different after metanoia or turning around. The scriptural story of Pentecost was one of the few stories I found that reflected my intuition that something remains still somehow incomplete even after all seems to be finished.[82] It hinted of a still yet-to-come shift in receiving Infinite Light and Love. I started to think that perhaps therein lay a clue to what happens when what seems to be journey's end turns out to be a new beginning.

I remembered I'd read somewhere that a Beloved will unravel your pockets so that, when your fingers go looking for what you have so carefully stored there, you'll find an empty pocket and need to return to the present.[83] I discovered that what I'd believed to be fleeting moments to be gathered into my pockets became instead moments of unending grace when I stopped storing them. My soul's song was no longer something I needed to reach out for or keep. It became instead Divine breath intimately filling me without need for form or place, an intimate encounter to receive—and to be received into.

> "I let myself receive Infinite Light and Love
> … opening me and opening to me so deeply.
> For when I genuinely love
> I wake up inside [Infinite Light and Love]" [84]

I KNEW, finally, that it was safe to be held and shaped by Spirit without needing to first hold and shape. On that day I opened my spirit to be embraced by the fire of the Light and Love that had brought us together in the first place and that now forever carried your fragrance. I didn't run out into the streets as did the apostles at Pentecost. I'm not even sure that the energy that filled me was visible to anyone other than me. I know though that it nevertheless still burns within me, though dimmer at some times than at others. Empty of the past I'd clung to and the future I'd imagined, everything is different now. I am no longer fettered by terror or fear of loss, at least not as before. Maybe I am coming closer to where the apostles danced that long ago day when they'd been filled with God's spirit.

Perhaps, in some small way much like that long ago day when Pentecost happened, Infinite Light and Love began to come to me differently, through you, my beloved friend, yet not from you. Then again maybe it wasn't Infinite Light and Love that came differently. Perhaps it was that I was finally able to turn around to receive Infinite Light and Love differently, no longer as something only true in what I could hold and touch, but as Divine breath filling me without need for form or place. I reflected on Pentecost with a changed perspective.

Scripture Meditation: Filled with Spirit (Acts 2:4)

> *I remembered the story of the day when the apostles experienced the fire and light of your spirit as they never had before. It wasn't that your Love and Light had not been present before that day. You had walked beside them and taught them every day. Even so, the apostles needed to be turned around, oriented to a world that had already been turned around for them. That day they received Spirit, not as they'd come to know it, but in its pure form.*
>
> *Everyone thought they were drunk. Perhaps they really were, drunk on the effervescence of pure Light and Love that carried your fragrance—and more—as it blew in, freeing them from their knowing and imagination, from all form and time. They were no longer energized by the adrenaline of fear ("what will happen to me?") or the excitement of mastery ("I've got it."), only by the joyous release of their soul's song, now forever held and protected in Spirit's embrace.*
>
> *It was no longer just about their human friendship with you, however divinely informed. It was about something much greater. They'd had a foretaste of this greater reality when they saw you transfigured. They'd*

tasted the joy then but didn't, I think, know how to allow it to hold them.

Now their soul's song—God's voice within—was finally and fully freed from human constraints. They knew as never before that neither human light nor darkness could overcome the essence of the Love and Light you'd carried within and shared so generously with them. Being a single (and singular) "other" witnessed from the outside no longer defined your reality. Now it shone without the limits of human dimensions, more than you yet still marked by your taste and scent. That day there was no longer any separation between them and God, or between them and you. They joined with and in God's very essence through you. They moved beyond what could be perceived through their five senses to what could only be conceived by the Holy Spirit.

Yielding: Dancing in Deepening Hope

Empty of the past I'd clung to and the future I'd reached out for, I am different now, forged by and forging deepening hope. Yielding became an inextricable part of receiving and being received into, as my understanding of surrender shifted and deepened. I stopped perceiving it as something I needed to will. I started to instead understand that the "I" I believed needed to will surrender was the very "I" that itself needed to yield to Infinite Light and Love. I realized that anything else was only a make believe surrender.[85] Paradoxically, I had not yielded even as I willed surrender. Now, surrender slowly became about yielding into Infinite Light and Love, the very soul—and song—of my reawakened self.

This realization blossomed one day, triggered by the startling thought that it was not, as I'd always thought, surrendering itself that I feared. In fact, I surrendered daily to fear and worry as well as to doubt and hopelessness. I surrendered almost as often to others' judgments, allowing them to increase my fears and doubts. Perhaps that was where and how I'd come to believe that surrender meant losing my self.

I reluctantly faced the truth: my reluctance to surrender was not about fearing surrender itself, rather it was about fearing who—or what—I surrendered to. Why did it seem so easy to surrender to fear yet so difficult to surrender to love, to worry and not to faith? The answer was evident yet not very palatable: I trusted fear and doubt and worry more than love or faith or hope. While neither desirable nor pleasant, fear and doubt were at least familiar and predictable. I knew their taste and shape and color inside and out. I knew how to "manage" them. They were my own creation. I could control them, though I always told myself I couldn't. Love and hope and faith, though, were much less familiar. I longed for them deeply yet I was much less conversant with them. They felt and indeed were somehow bigger than fear and doubt, more than I could create or control. I started to wonder if I'd ever really experienced anything other than only moments without fear doubt or worry.

As I was writing these words I remembered an earlier insight. My efforts to construct prose from well-worn pools of words and thoughts often resulted only in confounding and obscuring the reality I want to communicate. Those times taught me to wait for inspiration and then yield to it. This yielding had neither the quality of "giving up" or of "losing" I'd associated with surrender in the past, even though I could neither control nor create the inspiration to which I yielded. It happened only on its own time and in its own way. Could yielding to Beloved's Light and Love be more like allowing inspiration than I'd ever imagined? Perhaps that was the difference between perceiving surrender from my old familiar "hold on-let go" perspective where I held sway, and placing it within my new turned around perspective where it asked that I neither hold on nor let go but only that I simply yield.

I began to perceive such yielding as a participatory process true in both senses of that word: "giving in" and "bearing fruit." As I did, Infinite Love and Light became no longer something to be somehow taken or possessed however gratefully, nor to be possessed by, however willingly. They became instead about abundance inviting participation, not capitulation, about yielding, not possessing or submitting.

I don't fully understand what happened or how it happened. Perhaps I never will. What I do know is that I finally heard the distinction between a self *lost* and a self *loosened;* from a self lost, severed from itself, and a self loosened, released from the grip of all that held and defined it so tightly.

Surrendering—loosening—what had held me in bondage for so long, however frightening, was a "losing" I'd gladly embrace. Understood in this way, it was the natural outcome of yielding into what freed me, like a dancer yielding to the music that sets her heart to singing. It was in fact this very yielding that first called me to follow you, Beloved, though I had not known it then as I do now. I turned to scripture once again to reflect on words about surrender and imagined a conversation I might have had with you.

Scripture Meditation: Not As I Will, But As You Will (Matthew 26:39; Luke 22:42)

> *You always said it was about your Father's will, not your own. I felt a twinge every time I heard you say that. I heard a contradiction between the two. I didn't want to give up my will to follow you but neither did I want to give up yours. Your words began to truly resonate only when I shifted from perceiving your will as somehow an "object," something out there, separate and distinct, to perceiving it as "subject," love flowing within and through me.*

It was not about my will separate and severed from yours, enclosed by what I knew and wanted and imagined. It was about my will joined with yours—the music of Light and Love—resonating in my heart, yours yet mine, in me, given to me and in me.

KNOWING: Dancing in Deepening Faith

Simmering under both receiving and yielding was a KNOWING both forged by and forging deepening faith. It was a KNOWING that sang through my soul, telling of the essence of things, of Infinite Light and Love ever present not only in what is given to receive and yield into but also in me as me, somehow incarnate in my own human be-ing.

Grounded in this KNOWING I could now see that my journey was and always had been so much more than a means to an end, steps taken in order to reclaim my soul's song and taste heaven on earth. It had been and was instead about entering into a joyful dance with heaven on earth: all that is finite clothed in Infinite Light and Love; Infinite Light and Love clothed in the finite.

In the intimacy of receiving and yielding to wordless thoughtless Light and Love, KNOWING called me forth. It was the same KNOWING I had once been so certain of in my childhood. It was the wisdom of my soul's song, a deep sensing of the rhythm and nature of reality, so often present in childhood's innocence but then lost as that innocence itself is lost in the midst of acquiring external knowledge. The problem is not so much in acquiring the latter, I think, as in the belief that it must come at the expense of the former. I recalled something I'd read about the need to return to childhood's innocence, but with the wisdom of all we have experienced.[86] I now understood both the possibility and the reality reflected in that statement.

As more and more pieces fell into place I turned once again to the love story within which I'd found mirrors for so much of my journey. There I found echoes of this new-to-me conscious bearing of the love reflected in Beloved's gaze. I remembered a story of two women, Mary and Martha, close friends of Jesus. I'd always focused on the contrast between them, feeling somewhat guilty that I identified more with Mary than Martha. Now, I began to understand the story differently, as an example of the need for holding fast to the truth of Infinite Light and Love within and in all circumstances, whether "in the kitchen" or "at Jesus' feet." I imagined myself hearing their story once again, my heart awake to Beloved's love, hope and faith as if for the first time.

<u>Scripture Meditation: Mary and Martha (Luke 10: 40-42)</u>

> *I remembered all the times I'd heard the story of Mary and Martha. I'd focused on the externals, never really understanding why one woman was shamed in front of the other for simply asking for help, though perhaps she didn't do so in the most charitable way. Now, as I listened to it again, I started to believe that perhaps its message is not primarily about <u>what</u> each woman was doing but about <u>how</u> they were doing it. Each, in her own way, failed to bear the truth of Beloved's gaze amid contrasting external circumstances.*
>
> *Mired as Martha was in the complexity of preparing a dinner for a large group that included Jesus, her fear of losing the truth of Beloved's gaze is not surprising. I have experienced that as well. I know that, like her, I have often been distracted from the truth of Beloved's gaze as I am pulled by this and that. I don't hear Beloved's voice then. What I hear most loudly are the voices that echo what conditional love has taught me so well for so long and block the truth mirrored in Beloved's gaze.*

In seeming contrast, Mary sat at Jesus' feet, receiving and yielding to the love reflected in his gaze. Yet, she seemed to believe that the truth of his gaze was available and real only when immediate and physically present. Paradoxically, she too seemed to believe she would lose that truth. Apart from the external and immediate presence of her Beloved, she feared disconnection. I have experienced that fear also, implicit in my own reluctance to move away from the immediate and palpable presence of Beloved's gaze.

I wonder if Jesus, after responding to Martha and underlining the importance of bearing the truth of Beloved's gaze even amid the whirl of many responsibilities and tasks, didn't also have a quiet word with Mary. I dare to say this because I've been so like Mary at times and Beloved has had a word (or two) with me, reminding me that his voice comes in many forms.

Beloved, you invite me to dance the song of your presence my soul sings, whether next to you or through distance. You remind me that I am never apart from your gaze. Whether at your feet or mired in daily tasks, you tell me that I am always within your enduring embrace. There, I hear God's whispers most strongly. For that gift, I will always and forever say "Gracias."

Song Unending:

AFTER HAPPILY EVER AFTER

"Not knowing the true scale of things,
[we] imagine [we] have already arrived
when we are just beginning."
(E. Frankel)

Sometimes, we are "called not just to relocate to a new… land, but to cross over to an entirely new way of being."[87] These words heralded the new way station that lay beyond what I believed to be my last way station. I thought I'd reached my journey's apex as I reached the last way station. Love's call, which reawakened me to my soul's song, had come to me most strongly through the voice and presence of my beloved friend. Our deep friendship had drawn me on in times of joy as well as in times of confusion. With each step the music had grown sweeter and the melody more certain. I'd learned that even the silence between the notes could nourish and guide me.

Then, unexpectedly, my beloved friend passed away. Everything came to a stop in single moment like a needle being abruptly pulled off a vinyl record.[88] There was no longer either voice or physical presence. The silence was deafening. Darkness deeper than any I'd known before enveloped my heart. Even the silence *between* notes was gone for there were no more notes. Infinite Light and Love had come to me as gift wrapped in human skin and form. Now they offered their gift unwrapped. I was not ready.

My reception of Infinite Light and Love faltered. Without the light of my beloved friend's physical presence, I found myself blind. Like a sighted person who has learned to read braille yet still retains the option of reading print, I'd come to rely on external affirmation when my reception of my soul's song wavered. Now, all that remained to me were words written in braille. I wasn't sure I could read them fluently or that they were enough. I had no real idea of how to live *after* the happily ever after I'd come to know while my beloved friend had been physically present to offer reassurance and support. We're not told much about what comes after happily ever after. [89]

Fairytales end at happily ever after. Even scripture stories reflect this bias. There is one story in the Christian bible about a prodigal son who finds his way home after a long struggle. There he finds unexpected welcome and celebration and all ends "happily ever after." Nothing more is said about his return except for a few words from a jealous elder brother, and those are said to the father not the son. Presumably, all is now smooth sailing.

In some not fully conscious way, I'd always thought of *after happily ever after* as only an extension of what had been rather than a beginning of anything radically different. I'd expected that there would be fewer struggles and I'd somehow be able to negotiate those more easily. All would be forever well. In a way, that was true. In another way, I discovered, it was not true at all.

The storms of darkness I'd run into before had always ended and light had returned. Now, I could not imagine light returning. Earlier storms had taught me that light and darkness are both expressions of the singular reality of Infinite Light and Love in a 3-dimensional world. The storm that swirled around me now challenged that teaching. I could not in any way fathom the darkness around me now holding any expression of Infinite Light and Love.

Gradually, the outlines of this entirely new way station began to emerge. I was slowly drawn to deepen the spiral of love, hope and faith through three movements. The first, *Returning to Galilee*, invited me on re-member love's connection beyond its manifestation in human form and skin. The second, *Seeing Rightly*, invited me to experience hope beyond expectation, an ever-present body of energetic current living in the heart. The third, *Co-creating Song*, ushered me into faith as an act of voicing Infinite Light and Love's passionate exuberance, uniquely crafted for me and now free from the form I'd come to know when my friend had been physically present.

Each movement was both culmination and renewal of steps I'd carved out before, now walked in an entirely new way, no longer defined by a way station but more directly by the energies of love, hope and faith. (See reframed visual map)

REFRAMED VISUAL MAP

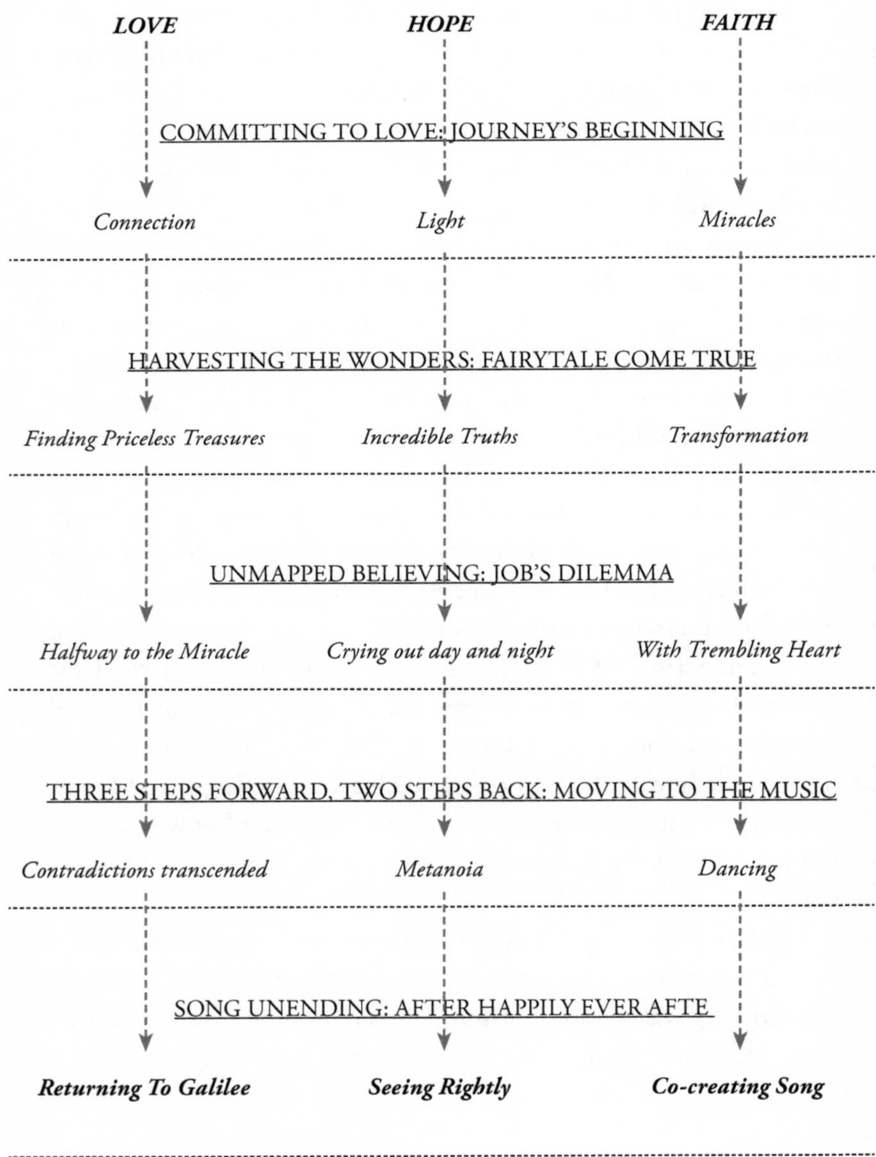

RETURNING TO GALILEE

"Whenever we are discouraged in our faith, whenever our hopes seem to be crucified, we need to go back to Galilee...back to the dream and the road ... that we had embarked upon before things went wrong."
(R. Rohlheiser)

The first movement of this way station became clear to me as I encountered the words quoted above. I got the message. Somehow, I needed to return to Galilee, to where, beyond time and form, the fire of friendship's hope and enthusiasm that had first reawakened my soul's song still burned brightly, undimmed by the loss of my friend's physical presence.

During times of separation in the past when my beloved and I could not stay in touch, I had become familiar with "kything," a type of spiritual tuning in to presence.[90] What I needed to do now was perhaps not so different. I re-read something I'd written earlier with new eyes: Love's mutuality insistently and tenderly urges me to stretch my limits and make space for the gift of Infinite Light and Love even when I do not feel like doing so or cannot comprehend how I might do so. There, I realized, was my route to "Galilee," where the essence if no longer the form of the love between my beloved friend and me awaited me.

I needed to turn toward that place once again (i.e., to re-turn) with increased awareness, persistence and intentionality. I'd had a foretaste of this practice before. It was not, however, simply about returning to what had been. I soon discovered the distinction between returning and re-turning. It is a distinction hinted at by both John O'Donohue and Jacque Lusseyran, as well as by Cynthia Bourgeault.

In his poem On the Death of the Beloved, O'Donohue says
"Let us not look for you only in memory,
Where we would grow lonely without you.
You would want us to find you in presence."[91]

Jacque Lusseyran, a blind hero of the French Resistance who wrote about blindsight,[92] echoes this same point: "In a spot like this [when you are separated from your Beloved], don't go too far afield for help. Either it is right near you, or it is nowhere."[93] He then advises us to look for a beloved who is no longer with us inside ourselves rather than out in the physical world.

Cynthia Bourgeault makes the same point even more emphatically:

"For none of the journey onward is possible if one is still subtly comparing it to the past, still waiting for a return [rather than a re-turn]...Next year's language is in next year's words. And one can hear them only if one is...aching wholeheartedly—body, mind, and spirit—toward the new arising, giving oneself totally and unreservedly into its hands."[94]

These words provided a path for me when I most needed it. I needed to ache wholeheartedly *not for the past* but for what was and always had been untouched by time or form. I needed to once again walk love's path, carved out across way stations. Each step once walked piece by piece—choosing connection, finding priceless treasures, being halfway to the miracle, transcending contradictions—I now needed to weave into a seamless whole.

As before, I turned to scripture and imagined myself among the apostles, hearing I needed to return to Galilee.

Scripture Meditation: Still Alive and Present *(Luke 24: 5,6; Matthew 28: 10)*

> *I remembered so clearly. My shock and grief at what had happened had not lessened one bit. I remember my fear that all I'd hoped for would now never be, that my journey had come to an end and our love itself was now only a memory. I wanted so badly to return to how it had been before.*

Just then I started to hear that all was not as I believed. I heard that you remained somehow still present and that we were to depart for Galilee, where we'd first met and fallen in love with you. You didn't ask us to remember Galilee. You asked us to return there.

I didn't want to return to Galilee, though, not at first. It was too painful to remember dreams I believed gone forever, much less to physically return to where they would be all the more vivid. I feared reliving what could no longer be. I kept getting caught in memory and grief. Yet, I also kept hearing your words to return.

Slowly, through my fears and tears, I begin to see a difference. It all hinged on a hyphen: re-membering, not remembering; re-turning, not returning. And so, I went, though at times my feet dragged.

To my utter surprise, you appeared to us in Galilee, just as you promised. You were not exactly as you'd been nor did we see you as frequently as we'd have liked. Nevertheless we did see you distinctly, more than a ghost or a disembodied remembrance. You were not physical yet somehow you were physical enough to eat with us and be touched by us.

I began to fully understand then why you asked us to go back to Galilee, "to the dream, hope, and discipleship that had once inflamed us."[95] *Only there could these be restored, not in the form into which we'd fashioned them as we walked with you, but in their essence, as you'd birthed them in us. There, at the core of Infinite Light and Love, all physical reality is quietly held, in exquisite fullness. There its promise is poised, ready to be poured out once more.*

SEEING RIGHTLY

"It is only with the heart that one can see rightly, what is essential is invisible to the eye." (St. Exupery)

The love, hope, and faith that inspired and led me throughout my journey remained whole in Galilee. Yet, regardless of how wonderful and inspiring the vision, nothing was quite as I'd known it. My mind's logic and reason repeatedly catapulted me out of Galilee, insistently asking how I could fully trust such a reality.

Galilee is the answer to love crucified. What is the answer to hope resurrected? How could I bear and stay open to hope returned, a resurrection my heart knew without question yet that remained beyond my mind's ability to perceive or comprehend? It took me a while to fully appreciate the challenge before me now, so similar to past ones yet radically different.

My return to Galilee highlighted the distinction between returning and returning once again. I began to perceive a second more subtle distinction enfolded within that one: the distinction between *going to* Galilee and *coming from* Galilee. Cynthia Bourgeault's words on unitive consciousness shed light on this distinction: "this 'inner wellspring' is no longer a place you go to; it's a place you *come from*."[96] My task now was to transcend binary mental constructs (e.g., here, there) and "see rightly" (i.e., beyond those constructs). Galilee was not a place in my mind's memory, out there somewhere. Rather it was, as it had always been, *present*, held within my heart, in me yet not contained or possessed by me.

I thought of Mary, listening to the angel Gabriel. I thought of Mary and Martha as against all odds their brother came back to life. These stories, like so many others, stop at "happily ever after." Little if anything is said about how these women trusted what their heart insisted invincibly was true. Nor is much said about how they yielded to the message of a world transformed beyond their wildest dreams, a message that so strongly contradicted all their minds could tell them was or could be possible.

It was love's light that, for me, first opened the door to Galilee when I'd reconnected with my beloved friend. It was love's light that now returned me to Galilee. I'd needed then to unbind love from the illusion of form. Now, it was hope I needed to unbind so that I could once again know it as a vibrant energy field in intimate communion with the reality my heart perceived.[97]

Unbound hope cancels fear. Fear ceases when we open, like trusting children, to hope's light, which navigates in and through relationship. The challenge is not so much to cease fearing. Rather it is to become "outrageously open:"[98] to unbind hope and allow our mind, which navigates through facts and logic and grows fearful when it cannot, to be enfolded into its light.

Earlier in my journey I'd written that when I surrendered in this way (i.e., opened outrageously), I received not an answer with sharply defined edges but an edge-less mystery that embraced me with a love beyond any that I had experienced or even imagined. I could understand now that it was a mystery held in and by hope's energy field. I thought again of the phrase that had haunted me from the start of my journey—"to make believing more than making believe." Such believing is well, if whimsically, described in the delightful little book *To Believe in God,*[99] in which it is likened to knowing such fantastical things as purple jelly beans hatching into ostriches and rabbits producing humans out of hats. In a way, seeing rightly involves equally incredible believing, inviting us to become outrageously open to an Infinite Light and Love so far beyond our mental constructs and paradigms that it defies comprehension and yes, even imagination.[100]

I re-traced the steps I'd taken following love, hope and faith, once taken one by one now a seamless whole. I remembered your teaching about becoming as a child and imagined talking with you about that.

Scripture Meditation: Becoming Like a Child (Matthew 18:3)

I remember all you asked us to believe and do: to love our enemies, to turn the other cheek, to forgive seventy times seventy, to not fear, to trust like the sparrows and the lilies. And I remember how often you welcomed the children.

I think maybe people have forgotten just how outrageously open children can be, how only such openness can truly embrace all you taught.

I suspect we didn't really understand just how outrageously open you asked us to be. I know I'd forgotten. Well, maybe not forgotten, but certainly not fully accepted. In some many ways I only made believe I believed. And that was OK for a long time, because you were always there to remind me, to model for me the reality of Infinite Light and Love. In your presence, what I believed to be impossible became possible: the blind could see and the lame could get up and walk. In your presence, my heart could soar. I could see rightly through your eyes.

Now, you are no longer here as before. Now, you ask that we see rightly through our own eyes; that we become outrageously open to Infinite Light and Love's incredible, impossible, outrageous reality and model it for others as you did for us. I'm not sure just how or even whether I can do that. But I will start.

CO-CREATING SONG[101]

There is an element of timeless creativity to seeing rightly that inspires a simultaneous engendering. (adapted from C. Bourgeault)[102]

It has been several years now since losing my friend's physical presence. It's been a time caught up in the challenge of seeing rightly, of sustaining as a living reality the gifts of love, hope and faith I received from my Beloved, both human and divine. The meaning of this challenge unfolded to a new level as I read Cynthia Bourgeault's words on the fourth "sense" of scripture: "The fifth-century Desert Father John Cassian once said that he knew that his monks had accessed [this sense] when 'they sang the psalms as if they were composing them.' "[103] At this level, Bourgeault asserts, we become not only "sensitive interpreters" of the patterns of wondrous mystery through which Infinite Light and Love speaks, but actual "*cocreators.*" [104]

Returning once again to Galilee, where my experience of Infinite Light and Love remains at its strongest, opened me to be once more bathed in its Spirit (i.e., love). Learning to see rightly opened my heart to Spirit's enduring presence (i.e., hope). Both now invited me to let that Spirit gush forth not only *through* me but *with* and *as* me. My challenge as I continued in this way station became no longer to simply hear, reclaim, and follow my soul's song, but to join my voice with it, giving it substance and weight so that it might take on unique form in time and space.

In *The Reed of God* Caryll Houselander likens Mary's virginity to the emptiness of a reed "through which Eternal Love was to be piped as a …song." He envisions each of us similarly, as a hollow reed, made "to receive the piper's breath" into form and time. Those words returned to me now. It is not about a passive receptivity though. It is, rather about an interactive, dialogic relationship, for it is who we are and how we are that gives visible form to Infinite Light and Love. In that sense we "co-create" the song of Infinite Light and Love carried by Spirit's breath.[105]

As I intuited this, I strived to understand it more fully. I turned to scripture's love story as I had so often before. There I found what I believe may be a hint of how that co-creation might be. At the last supper, Jesus asked those he loved and who loved him to do more than merely receive the gifts he offered. He challenged them to do something as incredible as hatching purple jelly beans into ostriches:[106] to transform bread and wine into their own living substance through their participation (i.e., to eat and drink them) and in so doing literally co-create his very being and unconditional love. I am not in any way denying the traditional theological significance and interpretation of Jesus' act. In focusing on that significance and interpretation, however, I know that I, and perhaps others as well, all too often remain unaware of just how outrageous, incredible and challenging his invitation to eat bread as his body and drink wine as his blood is. I imagined talking with Jesus about that.

Scripture Meditation: Do This in Remembrance of Me (Luke 22:19)

I was not at that last supper with you. I've only heard of your words—the words that puzzled, shocked and inspired those who heard them in person. As I hear them in my heart now what I hear is your invitation and challenge to literally re-member your presence—incarnate it in body and blood here on earth. Perhaps I hear them differently now because I too have lost a beloved friend. I did not know when I saw him for the last time that it would be the last time. I don't think the apostles knew either. They didn't call it a "last supper."

There is a difference between understanding the act of remembering as a recalling of someone or reliving something in memory, and knowing it as re-membering, a bringing back to wholeness what has been torn apart.[107] *I've read that it is a difference reflected in the Jewish word but not in the English word. The Jewish word, the word you spoke, is more similar to "invoke," to a witnessing (i.e., an action) that somehow reconstitutes a reality as still alive and present though not in the same form as before.*[108] *I think that's what you wanted us to understand: that it was the end of the story of Infinite Light and Love in one form yet its start as a story only just beginning to unfold in an entirely new form, a story we are meant to co-create, like reeds receiving your Spirit to issue it forth as song.*

Conclusion:

A POEM, A PRACTICE, AND SOME CLOSING THOUGHTS

"We don't get to heaven; we must become heaven"
(I. Zaleski)

DRAWN BY PRESENCE [109]

Drawn beyond presence, beyond my knowing
Drawn by a love remembered yet unimagined and unexpected
I stepped out into territory unexplored
I left home behind, thinking never to return

There, in the fields, I met my Beloved
There I lay enfolded in my Beloved's arms
Among the wildflowers
Fanned by my soul's song

Yet love beckoned me further still
I did not want to leave
Longing to remain within my Beloved's arms
I closed my eyes
Encircling all that was
Trying to hold it forever without change
Yet, grasped, the flowers faded
Bottled, my song grew silent

Afraid of loss, I became lost
I wandered into fields now silent and empty
There I longed for my Beloved's face
There I searched for my Beloved's touch

Finally, with nothing left to hold,
My arms fell open
In absence, love reached out without condition
In unknowing, hope unimagined gained voice
In surrender, faith without boundaries took shape
Love's call returned
(Perhaps it had never left)
I turned around

And saw my Beloved
My opened arms met open arms
My opened heart touched open heart
Amid wildflowers encircling us both

The reawakened notes of my soul's song returned to me
(or, perhaps, I returned to them)

LIFE AS *LECTIO DIVINA*

The words "beloved's gift" in the title of this book have multiple meanings. Two of those meanings were clear to me from the start: my beloved friend offered me the gift of his love, and he himself was gift from Divine Beloved. A third meaning, which I've come to treasure equally, became clear to me as I neared the completion of my writing: the gift, from both human and Divine Beloved, of a life practice. The realization of that practice, which remained an underlying and largely unconscious for many years, came as I read Christine Valters Paintner's *Eyes of the heart: Photography as Christian contemplation practice.*[110]

In this book Paintner proposes a visual practice parallel with *lectio divina*, an ancient Christian meditative practice for "being present to a sacred text in a heart-centered way."[111] "When we pray lectio," she says, "we see the words of scripture as God's living words being spoken to our hearts in this moment."[112] One day, as I read these words, which I'd read before, I saw them in a new way. I realized that the Way Stations that marked my journey had emerged from "reading" my life similarly, as Infinite Light and Love being spoken in and to my heart through particular experiences. *Lectio*'s four steps were clearly present once I realized this.

The first step involved attending to aspects of my experience that stood out in some way (i.e., that "shimmered" for me in Christine's words). At each way station I had reflected on the thoughts, experiences, feelings, sights or sounds that I had repeatedly been drawn to or been thinking about. For example, in my first Way Station, it was my commitment to love and how it was or was not playing out in my expectations of and response to my beloved friend that had most captured my attention. In my second Way Station, it had been the wonders of what I was experiencing that most called to me. And so on.

The second step was about staying present to those shimmering facets of my experience and tuning in to what they invited me to unfold within me. This step involved a time of both questioning and discernment. The balance between figuring out how I could make it better and discerning the voice of Infinite Light and Love within it was always a challenge that ultimately tipped toward the latter as my friend remained steadfast.

The next step then emerged in its own time. It involved asking, "What action/response is Infinite Light and Love inviting me to through this experience?" Clearer some times than others, this step often became the springboard for the next Way Station.

Finally, the fourth step was to simply rest before moving on, allowing the invitation to "marinate"[113] before taking any action. Interestingly, when I did that, the action often seemed to take itself.

This four-step practice evolved in an organic and largely intuitive fashion for a long time, shaping the sequence and content of each Way Station. It was not uncommon to find myself revisiting a Way Station I believed already completed: recommitting to love as I found myself in unmapped territory for example; or returning to harvesting wonders as I learned new steps to the back and forth rhythm of my soul's song. Severing one station from the other never worked. Getting caught up in the wonders without staying grounded in committing to love, for example, always distorted my perception of the wonders themselves. The full truth of each Way Station was only revealed as each both contributed to and received from the others.

SOME CLOSING THOUGHTS

Love is different from what I'd thought.

It is not just about connection and treasures.

It is also about traveling unmapped territory and, at times, moving two steps back for every three forward.

It is even about learning to live fully *after* happily ever after.

Hope is not about the expectation or achievement of desired outcomes.

It is about nurturing and cultivating that place in heart's depth where we meet and are met by Infinite Light and Love.

It is about tuning in to Infinite Light and Love as an abiding state of being. It involves embracing "the luminous fullness of the Land Promised to the Saints always and everywhere present beneath the surface motions of coming going, striving, arriving."[114]

Faith is not about fixed truths.

It is about living relationship.

It is active and reciprocal.

It is about co-creating soul's song into time and form.

Surrender is not about *what* we hold, but about *how* we hold it

My journey has been and continues to be ongoing prayer. Every day is both a continuation and a new beginning, another opportunity for me to weave heaven and earth into one and, perhaps more importantly, let myself be woven. Encouraged and accompanied by a love, hope and faith I'd once thought forever lost, I celebrate and pray with every breath:

> *I pray myself—and allow myself to be prayed.*
> *I pray love, as love was and is prayed for and with me;*
> *I pray hope, as hope was and is prayed for and with me; and*
> *I pray faith, as faith was and is prayed for and with me.*

When I started this journey inspired by deep friendship, I started on a journey I believed largely defined within the context of my relationship with a human beloved. Over time I've come to see that relationship as sacrament, a visible sign of relationship with Divine Beloved. As I have entered into the time when my human beloved is no longer physically present, I've realized even more deeply that my journey's essence is not, and never truly was, defined solely by its horizontal progression along a chronological timeline walked with another. It is, and always has been, most deeply defined by its vertical progression along the melody lines of my soul's song.

May my words inspire you to awaken to the melody lines of your own soul's song. May they lead you to the realization that, in the words of Tosha Silver, Infinite Light and Love is like an "ardent inner suitor … writing us love letters everyday," "constantly igniting roadside flares to get our attention"[115]

Endnotes

1 Thanks to Raimon Panikkar, from whom I have borrowed these words (used in his book *The Experience of God: Icons of the Mystery*, p.93*)* that so perfectly describe the format of this book.

2 Palmer, P. (2018). *On the brink of everything.* San Francisco, CA: Berrett-Koehler, p.4

3 Paintner, C. V. (2013). *Eyes of the heart: Photography as a Christian practice of contemplative practice*, p. 33.

4 The practice of life from/through this perspective is described in more detail in the book's Conclusion

5 Katie, B. (2017). *A mind at home with itself.* NY: HarperCollins, p. 238.

6 O'Donohue, J. (1997). *Anam Cara: A book of Celtic wisdom*. NY: Harper Collins, p. 8

7 I no longer remember where I first read about these communities. Since then though I have found reference to something similar in a book by Mia Kalef, who tells of couples singing a song as they make love and then teaching it to the village elders so that they can sing it to their baby at birth.

8 Shulman, J. (2006). *The instruction manual for receiving God.* Boulder, CO: Sounds True.

9 I believe that these gazes and acceptance come in some way for all children though for some they come not from people but from creation, animals and nature.

10 Kent, C. and Pintauro, J. (1968). *To Believe in God.* NY: Harper & Row

11 The term "homemade self' has been used by Fr. Thomas Keating to describe our self-created identity. I prefer it to "ego," as it is both more descriptive and carries fewer negative connotations.

12 I use this phrase—Infinite Light and Love—interchangeably with God. For me it describes the essence of God as I experience God, without gender, image or imagination

13 Block, P. (2003). *The answer to how is yes.* San Francisco, CA: Berrett-Kohler, p. 24

14 O'Donohue, J. (1997). *Anam Cara: A book of Celtic wisdom*

15 Told to me by my friend Trudy Schoepko, source not known.

16 Analogously, there are two ways to swim: by sheer effort, out of touch with the nature of water ("us against the water") OR as one with its nature ("us with the water").
17 See previous footnote for definition of term
18 N. Kazanzakis (1968)
19 Leloup, J-Y. (1986) *The Gospel of Thomas*, p. 63
20 Salzberg, S. (2003). *Faith: Trusting Your Own Deepest Experience*, p.81
21 Ibid
22 Wink, W. (1992). *Engaging the Powers*
23 Ibid, p. 309
24 Ibid, p. 103
25 This phrasing is inspired by Salzberg, S. (2003).
26 based on Douglas-Klotz' translation of Our Father in *Prayers of the Cosmos* (1993)
27 L'Engle, M. (1978). *The Weather of the Heart*, p. 45
28 Leloup, J-Y. *Gospel of Mary Magdalene*. Rochester, VT., p. 125
29 Newell, P. *Book of Creation*, p. 9
30 Kenneth White, cited in Newell, *Book of Creation*, p.9
31 Bourgeault, C. *Love Is Stronger than Death*, p. 92
32 Ibid, p. 92
33 Megan McKenna, from a handwritten poem given to me many years ago when we were both in college
34 Wording from *The Message*
35 Rohlheiser, R. (2001), *Against an infinite horizon: The finger of God in our everyday life*, NY: Crossroad Publishing
36 Ibid, p.74
37 Ibid, p.75
38 A delightful story of love's power to transform is told by Stephen Mitchell's in his adaptation of the classic fairy tale, *The frog prince: A fairy tale for consenting adults*. The opening quote to this section is taken from this book.
39 Bonder, N. (1999) *Yiddishe Kop: Creative Problem Solving in Jewish Learning, Lore and Humor*
40 According to Jewish tradition, Nachson, a man who didn't know how to swim, had to jump into the Red Sea before it would part. His story is recounted in Bonder, N. (1999), *Yiddishe Kop: Creative Problem Solving in Jewish Learning, Lore and Humor*, p. 82
41 In *Boehme for Beginners* CD series (C. Bourgeault)

42 *Listen: Finding God in Your Life*; KW Kent, San Francisco, CA: Jossey-Bass, p.40

43 It seemed like saying Yes was a message that kept finding me (e.g., Block's *The answer to how is yes*; Ryan's *Praying dangerously: Radical reliance on God*)

44 Salzberg, S. *Faith*, NY: Riverhead Books, p. 175-176

45 I am indebted to Ellen Davis' wonderful book *Getting Involved with God* for my understanding of Job's dilemma

46 Block, P. (2001). *The Answer to How is Yes*. San Francisco, CA: Berrett-Koehler, p. 24

47 Davis, E. (2001). *Getting Involved with God*, p. 127. Cambridge, MA: Cowley Publications

48 Shaia, A. *Beyond the Biography of Jesus: The Journey of Quadratos* Book I, Nashville, TN: Cold Tree Press, p.71

49 Paraphrase of a statement in Nouwen's *Turn My Mourning Into Dancing*: "Loving someone means allowing the other person to respond in ways you have no control over" (p.28).

50 These questions, exempting the last one, come from Peter Block's *The Answer to How Is Yes* (2002), p. 34-36

51 Quoted in Barry, W., *A friendship like no other*, p. 127, Chicago, IL: Loyola Press

52 Block, P. (2001). *The Answer to How is Yes*. San Francisco, CA: Berrett-Koehler, p. 27

53 Shaia, A. (2006). *Beyond the Biography of Jesus: The Journey of Quadratos Bk I*, p. 71

54 Ryan, S.R., *Praying dangerously: Radical reliance on God*, p.vii

55 Used in M. Lucado's *Every Day Deserves a Chance* (2008)

56 Only much later l did I realize that this persistent need to know how was at the root of the distinction between the parable of the rich young man and that of Bartimeus the blind beggar (see reflection in Part I on Asking to See).

57 Wiederhehr, M. (2011). *Abide: Keeping Vigil with the Word of God* Collegeville, MN: Liturgical Press, (Kindle Loc 721)

58 This understanding of surrender is echoed in a 6/21/18 blog post by Nipon Mehta on www.gratefulness.org in which he says "surrender isn't a sacrifice of the known but rather a celebration of the infinite."

59 Yaconelli, M. (2002). *Dangerous spirituality: God's annoying love for imperfect people*, Grand Rapids, MI: Zondervan, p. 34

60 Inspired by and loosely adapted from St. John of the Cross' Dark Night poem

61 Found in Mark Batterson's book *The Circle Maker.*

62 Chittister, J. (2010). *Illuminated life: Monastic wisdom for seekers of light*

63 Phrase used in Kent, C. and Pintauro, J. *To Believe in God*

64 Merton, T. *Conjectures of a Guilty Bystander*. NY: Harper & Row

65 Contained in one of series of email reflections by Fr. Ron Rohlheiser <ronrohlheiser.com>

66 Shaia, A. *Beyond the Biography of Jesus: The Journey of Quadratos, Bk II.* Shaia is one of the few writers I found who talk about the "after the happily ever after" phase of spiritual journeying

67 The parts of this paragraph that are in quotes are from Newell's *Cosmic Christ* which I've chosen/adapted to fit my own interpretations of them.

68 Barron, R. *And Now I See* (1998)

69 Bonder, N. (1999). *Yiddishe Kop: Creative Problem Solving in Jewish Learning, Lore and Humor* (see endnote #40)

70 Told in O'Donohue, J. (2009). *Anam Cara*. NY: Harper Perennial

71 Gracias for you steadfastness, beloved friend. That has become sacrament also.

72 Finley, J. (1999). *The Contemplative Heart*

73 Insight inspired by Barry,W.A. (2011). *Changed Heart, Changed World: The Transforming Freedom of Friendship with God.* Chicago, IL: Loyola Press

74 This distinction is not often addressed. One of the best discussions of believing without really believing that I've read can be found in *Insurrection* by P. Rollins, which I ran across only after I'd written this material.

75 As put by R. Rohr in *The Naked Now*

76 See earlier reflection in Choosing Light

77 Gracias, beloved friend.

78 Allender, D. (2010). *Sabbath*. Nashville, TN: Thomas Nelson, p.31

79 Finley, J. Cloud of Unknowing video posted on www.thecontemplativeway.org

80 Metaphor used in Frazier, J. (2012). *The freedom of Being at Ease with What Is.* NY: Weiser Books

81 Quoted in *Boehme for Beginners* CD series (Cynthia Bourgeault, Contemplative Society)

82 As it turned out this was only the first step in reflecting on the meaning of Pentecost. See Co-creating Song in Song Unending section

83 Frazier, J. (2012). *The freedom of Being at Ease with What Is*. NY: Weiser Books. For grounding this understanding, gracias Beloved.
84 Paraphrased from Symeon the New Theologian as cited in *The holy Trinity and the law of three*, C. Bourgeault, p.175.
85 One of the most beautiful descriptions of surrender I've heard is given by James Finley as he talks about watching a sunset in *Trauma and Spirituality*, a CD series with Carolyn Myss
86 Chilson, R.W. *Yeshua of Nazareth: Spiritual Master*
87 Frankel, E., *The wisdom of not knowing*. Boulder, CO: Shambala, p.16-17
88 The sound of a needle being abruptly pulled off a record is unforgettable for those familiar with vinyl records. It also scratches the record badly so don't try it with a new record if you are only now becoming familiar with vinyl!
89 An interesting (though not totally analogous) perspective on after happily ever after is described by Alexander Shaia in a chapter titled *The Fourth Path: Walking on Luke's Road of Riches* in his book *The Journey of Quadratos*
90 Savary, L. M. & Berne, P. H., (1988) *Kything: The art of spiritual presence. Mahwah,* NJ: Paulist Press
91 O'Donohue, J. (2008). *To bless the space between us*. NY: Doubleday, p. 170
92 See earlier discussion in Moving to the Music way station
93 Lussyran, J. (2006). *And there was light*. Sandpoint, ID: Morning Light Press. p. 259
94 Bourgeault, C., *Love is stronger than death*, p.58
95 Rohlheiser, R., *Where to find resurrection*. www.ronrolheiser.com
96 Bourgeault, C. (2016) T*he heart of centering prayer: Nondual Christianity in theory and practice*, Boulder, CO: Shambala, p.135
97 C. Bourgeault elaborates on this idea of hope in her book, *Mystical Hope*
98 Thanks to Tosha Silver's *Outrageous openness: Letting the divine take the lead* (2016) for this wonderful phrase and concept
99 Kent, C. and Pintauro, J. (1968). *To Believe in God*. NY: Harper & Row
100 Paraphrased from Van Praagh, J & Johnston, S. D. *When Heaven Touches Earth*
101 It is, I think, fitting that the title and substance of this last reflection was inspired by words from Cynthia Bourgeault. Her courageous book, *Love is stronger than death*, offered me my first map for my own inner journey. Now, in this last way station, words from another of her books, *The wisdom way of knowing: Reclaiming an ancient tradition to awaken*

the heart, offered me guidance once again. Amazingly, I also just recently found a similar affirmation of co-creation in *Jazz, Evolution and Co-Creation with the Trinity* (www.omegacenter.info, March 4, 2019)

102 Original quote: "There is an element of primordial timelessness to unitive seeing, as the seeing becomes simultaneously an engendering."

103 Bourgeault, C. (2003). *The wisdom way of knowing: Reclaiming an ancient tradition to awaken the heart.* San Francisco. CA: Jossy-Bass, p.95

104 Ibid

105 An article in Omega Center's 3/4/2019 blog, *Jazz, Evolution and Co-Creation with the Trinity,* offers another fascinating metaphor for the kind of co-creation I've intuited (see footnote above)

106 This image from *To Believe in God* (Kent, C. and Pintauro, J.) is one of my favorite ones for communicating just how incredible Jesus' invitation truly was, and is

107 Definition given by Newell, J. P. (*Remembering the past, re-membering the future.* Huffington Post, 11/9/2011)

108 This is my interpretation based on several internet references on the Jewish understanding of remembrance

109 My translation and loose adaptation of St. John of the Cross' poem Dark Night

110 Frederick Buechner's *The Remarkable Ordinary,* which I was not familiar with as I wrote this book, also speaks to this type of practice, though in a much less formalized fashion

111 Paintner, C. Valters (2013). *Eyes of the heart: Photography as a Christian contemplative practice.* Notre Dame, ID: Sorin books, p.33

112 Ibid

113 Thanks for this wonderful image, Rachel Slagle Pearson

114 Bourgeault, C. (2001) *Mystical hope: Trusting in the mercy of God.* Boston, MA: Cowley, p.18.

115 Inspired by and quoted from Tosha Silver's *Outrageous openness: Letting the Divine lead you*, p. 8. Thank you, Tosha.

CPSIA information can be obtained
at www.ICGtesting.com
Printed in the USA
BVHW081116240419
546394BV00005B/486/P

9 781982 224462